The Daily Telegraph

INVESTING IN A SECOND HOME

WENDY PASCOE

A practical guide for would-be property investors – holiday lets, long and short letting, student accommodation

2ND EDITION

howtobooks

BUYING A PROPERTY IN SCOTLAND AND NORTHERN IRELAND

Buying a property in Scotland or Northern Ireland is different in several respects to the system used in England and Wales. In Scotland, for example, on a fixed price property, the seller will take the first offer received for that amount. And in Scotland, many properties are bought via Solicitors' Property Centres rather than estate agents usually found elsewhere. In Northern Ireland, differences there include the vendors arranging searches and the fact that contracts are accepted and not exchanged. And there are further differences in the purchase procedures.

The purpose of this book is to look at property investment strategy and not to provide a comprehensive guide to the differences between the various systems. Generally, the English model has been used when referring to property purchases and court procedures. If you are in doubt about the procedures and implications of buying in Scotland or Northern Ireland, or even Wales, then it is important to seek professional advice from solicitors in those areas.

Published by How To Books Ltd,
Spring Hill House, Spring Hill Road
Begbroke, Oxford OX5 1RX
Tel: (01865) 375794. Fax: (01865) 379162
email: info@howtobooks.co.uk
http://www.howtobooks.co.uk

First edition 2004
Second edition 2006

British Library Cataloguing in Publication Data
A catalogue record for this book is available from the British Library

ISBN 10: 1 84528 138 1
ISBN 13: 978 1 84528 138 0

Cover design by Baseline Arts Ltd, Oxford
Produced for How To Books by Deer Park Productions, Tavistock
Illustrations by Nicki Averill
Typeset by PDQ Typesetting, Newcastle-under-Lyme, Staffs.
Printed and bound in Great Britain by Bell & Bain Ltd., Glasgow

NOTE: The material contained in this book is set out in good faith for general guidance and no liability can be accepted for loss or expense incurred as a result of relying in particular circumstances on statements made in the book. The laws and regulations are complex and liable to change, and readers should check the current position with the relevant authorities before making personal arrangements.

Contents

Acknowledgements   xi

Introduction   xii

1 · Why Buy an Investment Property?   **1**
Can you afford it?   3
Long lets versus holiday lets   4
How to calculate your yield   5
Timescale: are you in it for the long run?   7
Your acceptable level of risk   9
Void periods   11
Your valuable time   11
Potential disasters   13
Crystal ball gazing   14

2 · Raising the Money   **16**
Recent history...   16
...and what changed   17
When to go for advice   18
Where to go for advice   19
Raising money: the options   21
Type of mortgage   29
What lenders will want from you   30
Do not borrow more than you can afford   31
Do not get too hung up on mortgages   32

3 · The Right Property   **34**
Long lets   35
Holiday lets   35
The importance of research...   36
...and how to do it   37
Who looks for the property   40
Where to buy   41
What to buy   43

Inheriting property   46
Pros and cons of buying an existing rental property   46
City developments and loft living   47
How to buy your property   49
Searches   51
Surveys   52
Neighbours   52

4 · Who Needs an Agent Anyway?   **54**
What long-lettings agencies do   55
How to find a decent agent   57
Agency charges   58
Should you go it alone?   58
The agent's role in helping set the rent   61
What holiday lettings agencies do   62
How to find a decent agent   63
Agency charges and conditions   66
Should you go it alone?   67
Pricing your holiday letting property   71

5 · How to Market Your Property   **74**
Long letting   74
Holiday letting   77
Market research   78
Methods of marketing your property   82
Budgeting for your marketing campaign   90
Why you probably need a brochure   90
The importance of a mailing list   91
Repeat bookings   92
Is it all worth it?   93

6 · The Long-letting Landlord   **94**
Furnished versus unfurnished   94
Minimum to provide if you furnish   96
Getting ahead of yourself   99
Tenancy Agreements   99

What to include in a Tenancy Agreement   102
Cleaning and decorating   109
Routine maintenance   111
Corporate letting   111
Disabled access   112
Why it is important to keep good tenants   113
How to keep your tenants happy   113

7 · Furnishing a Holiday Cottage   116
How to decorate   117
How much to spend   118
What to buy   119
Stockists   134
The garden   135

8 · Cleaning a Holiday Cottage   137
The importance of a routine   138
A recommended system   139
The cleaning   141
Less frequent jobs   147
Fortnight visitors   147

9 · Managing a Holiday Cottage   149
Merits of a personal welcome   150
What guests expect on arrival   150
Optional extras   151
Food   153
Guests' information folder   154
Additional services to offer   157
What guests expect during their holiday   157
Who pays for breakages?   159
Who does the cleaning?   160
Closing down for winter   161
What to ban   161

10 · Buying for Student Children — **164**

How to raise the money — 166

What to buy — 169

How to furnish the property — 170

Who manages the property — 172

Security — 174

When to sell the property — 176

Tax and how to pay less of it — 177

11 · Rules, Regulations and Legalities — **179**

Before you let for the first time — 180

Gas — 180

Oil — 182

Solid fuel stoves/open fires — 182

Ventilation: flues and chimneys — 183

Electricity — 183

Upholstered furniture — 185

General safety: protecting yourself — 185

Smoke detectors and carbon monoxide detectors — 186

Fire extinguishers and fire blankets — 186

Houses in Multiple Occupation (HMOs) — 187

Private water supplies — 188

Fines and prison — 188

Who to check your obligations with — 188

Remembering your obligations — 188

Risk assessments — 189

Property covenants or other restrictions — 189

The agent's contract with you — 190

Insurance — 196

Council tax and business rates — 199

12 · What To Do If It All Goes Wrong — **201**

Prevention is better than cure — 202

Who is the boss? — 203

How to spot early signs of trouble — 203

Verbal and written warnings — 205

Serving notice   208
Going to court   208
Holiday letting properties   212
If *you* get something wrong   213
How to deal with complaints   214

13 · Money Out   **217**
Buying costs   218
Selling costs   221
After you have bought the property   221
Agency or marketing costs   222
Furnishing costs   223
Running costs – long letting   224
Running costs – holiday letting   224
Repairs and renewals   225
Administrative costs   226
VAT   227
Capital gains tax   227

14 · Money In   **229**
How the system works   230
What is an allowable expense?   232
How to set out your expenditure   235
What to do with your receipts   237
Other methods of arranging your tax   237
How to set out your income   238
What to do with your income and expenditure details   239
Roll over relief and capital gains   240
Pension contributions   240
Overseas owners   240

15 · Building Your Empire   **242**
Spreading your risk   243
How to borrow money to finance your portfolio   244
There is nothing wrong with borrowing   246
How to use the system to acquire multiple properties   248

Selling versus refinancing   250
How much is it possible to borrow?   251
What happens if property prices fall?   251
Do lenders mind who you let your properties to?   252
What to buy   252
Could you be a property developer?   255
Marketing   257
Long-term trends and your portfolio   257

Appendix 1 – Checklist for furnishing your long let   *260*
Appendix 2 – Checklist for furnishing your holiday let   *262*

Index   *269*

Acknowledgements

Thank you to everyone who helped compile this book, and the endless patience they showed.

Particular thanks to Tristan Bishop of Peter A Bishop and Andy Darroch of Compass Associates who advised me on money, mortgages and other financial matters; accountant Robert Cowie of Winter Rule on tax, student letting and money generally; Stephen Fenton of Homequest Property Management and Malcolm Harrison of the Association of Residential Letting Agents (ARLA) on lettings; Brian Adair of Ryden Lettings in Edinburgh, who is also ARLA's Scotland chairman, on letting in Scotland; and Phil Jelley of Legal Insurance Management and Rory Walker of Holiday Cottages Insurance (a division of Henderson & Co) on insurance.

Thanks also to Simon Tregoning and Suzanne Woodward of Classic Cottages for their advice on holiday letting; Jane Woolcock, also on holiday and long lettings; and Neil Sergeant of Stratton and Holborrow and Ludvic Laskowski of Lillicrap Chilcott for their advice on property purchases and auctions; Eleanor Clark of HomePoint, Communities Scotland, for advice on buying property in Scotland; Gareth Hardwick of the National Landlords Association; and Zahid Hussain of The Money Centre.

And thank you finally to my volunteer reading group of Chris, Lorna, Sarah and Sue for their constructive criticism.

Introduction

Investing in property has never been easier and more popular. You can borrow money by picking up the phone; savings accounts often pay modest interest rates; the potential for long term capital growth is good, and pensions and investment-backed products have had, to put it mildly, a roller coaster few years.

Investors, especially those starting out, like property. It is tangible: you can go and look at your asset and touch it and manage it yourself. Unlike shares, its fate is not directly in the hands of the traders on the stock markets of London, New York or Tokyo. Of course like any speculative investment there is always risk, and what goes up may come down, but if you are in it for the long term then that risk is reduced.

This book looks at the practical side of investing in property, the rules and regulations you need to know, and what to do if it all goes wrong.

But if you were never keen on homework this may not be the project for you. If you are not prepared to put in the preparatory work (or pay someone to do it for you) and end up with the wrong property, then it could become a financial millstone which could drag you and your family under and leave you with debts that will take a lifetime to clear.

1

Why Buy an Investment Property?

Property is a national obsession, taking over from the weather as our favourite topic of conversation. Once it was about property prices and how our homes earned more than we did just by sitting there. Now it is about squeezing value from property, so that means renovations and rebuilds, makeovers, Buy to Let and even portfolio building. Whole television series are devoted to the subject, but sadly it is never quite as easy as it seems in a half hour programme.

The first question to ask yourself is what you want out of the project. The answer should not be because everyone else seems to be doing it or because it seems like an easy way to make money. If everyone else really is doing it then that is the time to do something else: if it is easy money you are after then go out and buy a lottery ticket.

The reason you need to decide on your motives first is because it will decide everything else: ie when you invest, the type of property you buy, what you put in it, and who your target guests or tenants will be. Ask yourself:

◆ Do you want a regular income from your second property?
◆ Are you hoping the property will increase in value?
◆ Do you want both income and capital growth?
◆ Is it because you believe the property market is continuing to rise and you want to stay part of it?
◆ Have stock market uncertainties deterred you from investing in shares, and you want a safer return on your money?
◆ Have low interest rates meant a poorer return on your savings and you want the chance of improving on them?
◆ Do you want to invest in property to help boost your ailing pension?
◆ Do you want a second home principally for you, your family and friends to use, with the opportunity of making a bit of extra money on the side?
◆ Is it likely you may ever live in the property yourself?
◆ Do you want to holiday let?
◆ Do you want to long let?
◆ Do you want to invest in property on behalf of your student son or daughter?

And some personal questions to ask yourself:

◆ How much research am I prepared to do?
◆ How much money am I prepared to risk?
◆ Do I want a quick return or am I in it for the long term?

The huge rises in house prices in the last few years are still fresh in many people's minds, and it is tempting to assume they will soon be back. But common sense tells you this is unlikely – at least in the short term – and that it would be investor-suicide to rely on it.

CAN YOU AFFORD IT?

The odd thing about mortgages is that the maximum amount you can borrow is often dependent on your salary or earnings and not what you can afford. Earnings and affordability are not the same thing at all.

For example, family A earns a total of £60,000 a year. Family A is a married couple with no children. They do not drink, smoke or take exotic foreign holidays and have a small mortgage outstanding on the family home. Family B earns the same, yet this couple has two children (one at private school, one at university), smoke and drink socially, who ski in February and take a long-haul beach holiday each summer. Family B recently remortgaged the family home to raise money for a loft conversion. On paper, the two families should be able to borrow about the same, but in practice who can afford the larger loan?

Increasingly, lenders are recognising that affordability and lifestyle may be a better guide to who can afford what. So when you do your own calculations, take into account that same affordability factor.

In many cases your investment property will be self financing, that is the rent will cover the mortgage. But it is still important to consider the affordability factor because:

- your borrowing may depend on it (especially if you are remortgaging your family home)
- you will have to pay legal fees, stamp duty and possibly agent or search fees
- you will have to spend money on preparing your property for letting (renovations or repairs)
- you will have to spend money on decorating and perhaps furnishing your property.

In short, you need to calculate how much spare cash you have each month until your investment property is up and running and self-financing.

LONG LETS VERSUS HOLIDAY LETS

If your purpose in investing in a second property is just to make money and you have no preference about the type of property, location or tenant, then you can choose between a holiday letting cottage or apartment or a property which is long let, ie usually on a fixed contract of six months or over.

Points to consider include:

- *Holiday or short term letting* will almost certainly bring you in more income.
- But you will have to pay all the bills. These will include buildings and contents insurance, council tax, electricity, gas, oil, water, TV licence, holiday lettings' agency fees, laundry and ironing bills, cleaner and gardener.
- You have to furnish a holiday let.
- However, all the above costs are tax deductible.
- You can still use the property yourself and take holidays there.
- You do not hand over control of it to tenants.

- *Long lets* may make you less money.
- But the only bills you will probably have to pay are buildings insurance (and the regular servicing of appliances, which you would have to anyway with a holiday let).
- You do not have to furnish a long let.

If after having done your sums it is still too close to call then consider that holiday letting has the *potential* to be more troublesome, if only because your tenants change every week or fortnight and they will expect high standards. With a long let, assuming your tenants are not arsonists, own a pack of large dogs, or have twelve children sleeping in two rooms, you have a reasonable chance of getting decent ones who will look after your property as well as can be expected.

Also consider whether you, your family or friends may want to use your investment property for holidays or short breaks. If so, then clearly the answer is to invest in a holiday cottage in a good area you want to stay in, rather than a property in a town centre or close to a business park.

The same applies if you think it is ever likely you may want to live in your investment property, for example if you are close to retirement, are considering down-sizing from your current family home, or just want to relocate to a different part of the country.

HOW TO CALCULATE YOUR YIELD

Whatever your purpose in investing in a second property, the type or its location, you will need at some stage to calculate your likely yield or return. The yield is simply what rent or income you receive in relation to the money you have invested, usually expressed as a percentage.

Calculating yield is important because:

◆ It will help you compare the returns on different properties.
◆ It will help you compare the return on your investment in the letting property with, for example, what the same money could achieve in a savings account.
◆ It will help you compare the return on your property with what inflation is doing (ie, whether your money is better off under a mattress).

There are several methods of calculating yield. There is no industry standard, but one of the most common ways is for annual rent to be expressed as a percentage of the value of the property at current prices. For example:

Property is worth:	£120,000
Monthly rent:	£500
Total rent per annum:	£6,000
Annual yield:	5%

(Calculate yield by dividing annual rent by property value and multiplying by 100.)

Other options are variations on the same theme:

◆ Annual rent expressed as a percentage of how much you paid for the property.
◆ Annual rent expressed as a percentage of the cash deposit put down when the property was purchased.

Gross yield is income from the property with nothing deducted (as in the above example).

Net yield is income from the property after expenses have been deducted, including mortgage interest, insurance, agency fees, repairs and maintenance and so on. With net yield the above example could look like this:

Property is worth:	£120,000
Monthly rent:	£500
Total rent per annum:	£6,000
Less expenses:	£1,200
Equals:	£4,800
Annual yield:	4%

(Total rent less expenses, divided by property value and multiplied by 100.)

In the last few years some investors were lucky enough to see double digit yields from their properties, helped by low property prices (especially in the north) and relatively high rents. Unfortunately, far fewer investors will enjoy those levels of returns in the near future. Instead, a rental property yielding perhaps 4–8% a year gross and 2–4% a year net would be rather more realistic.

But remember that these yield calculations do not include the chance of future rises in the value of your property. Many investors may decide that capital growth over the long term is their primary aim and yield is of only secondary importance: nice if it is there but not important.

TIMESCALE: ARE YOU IN IT FOR THE LONG RUN?

There is an argument that says that as long as you are able to hold onto your investment properties indefinitely then peaks and troughs in the market in the meantime do not matter because (fingers crossed) *virtually all property is bound to rise in value eventually*. The problem with this approach is that you can never foresee when you may have to sell, for example if you need the money unexpectedly for something else.

Whatever your own views, there is no doubt that the longer you are in the market the safer your investment will probably be. Organisations such as ARLA (the Association of Residential Letting Agents) calculate a medium- to long-term investment should be typically over 15–20 years. You may be lucky and be able to turn around a property in six months and walk away with a profit, but guessing the market that accurately probably says more about your luck and your willingness to take a risk than your business acumen.

Happily though, the lettings market and property booms are often what are called counter-cyclical. This means they are doing different things at different times, and regardless of what point we are in the cycle you (the landlord) should benefit. For example, house prices usually only fall if nobody is buying them. If nobody is buying them then more people are renting and demand will squeeze supply which pushes rents higher. But rising property prices will encourage more landlords into the market which will increase supply and rents will fall. In the meantime the high property prices will encourage many small landlords to sell for a quick profit and the whole thing starts over again.

But if you are determined to do it for the short term:

◆ Do not take on properties which need a lot of building work unless you have access to a 100% reliable architect, builder and project manager.

- Make sure you know your local market inside out and be
  confident that you can sell for a big enough profit in order to:
  – cover your buying and selling costs, including stamp duty
  – cover whatever you have spent on renovations, decoration
  and furnishings
  – still make you a profit on top of all your expenses.
- Avoid holiday letting properties which may need significant
  sums spent on them (decorating and furnishing to a high
  standard) which you probably will not be able to recoup in the
  short term.

YOUR ACCEPTABLE LEVEL OF RISK

There is no point investing in a second property if you are going to
have sleepless nights every time property prices wobble, when
interest rates move or when a tenant breaks the boiler. *You have to
be comfortable with a degree of uncertainty, especially if you have
stretched yourself financially.*

But there are some ways of guaranteeing a more regular income:

- Some private residential developments offer investors what are
  described as guaranteed returns on their money over a specified
  period, usually the first one or two years. Essentially it is a carrot
  from the developer to attract buyers. Look carefully at any terms
  offered: you may well do better renting on the open market, but
  this has to be balanced out by the benefits of a regular income
  which may be especially useful in the early years by offsetting the
  buying and setting up costs you incurred.

- Some holiday home complexes also offer guaranteed returns for
  the first couple of years. Look carefully at the annual charges
  which could include ground rent, maintenance and management
  fees, electricity and water bills. Make sure one does not cancel

the other out, but again that peace of mind in the first year or two may be worth having.

◆ Some local authorities also offer guaranteed rent schemes for an initial period of up to about three years. They also guarantee to return the property to you in its original condition, minus any acceptable wear and tear. Again, the rent they offer may be less than the going rate but this has to be balanced out by the advantages of a steady income. Some mortgage companies will not lend on properties which will be let to local authorities or housing associations.

◆ Contact large local employers in your area, for example hospitals or universities. Many organisations like these, which have a fast turnover of staff, maintain their own lists of suitable rental properties and are sometimes prepared to guarantee rents in order to ensure availability. This is commoner in areas where there is a shortage of quality, rented accommodation.

◆ If you are planning to holiday let, speak to potential letting agencies as soon as possible. Ask which areas they prefer, the type of property and the number of weeks a year they would anticipate filling. Most reputable agencies have good websites, so go online and check their bookings' records as well.

◆ For long lets do the same. Speak to residential agencies. Can they line up tenants in advance? (Usually it is no further ahead than four or five weeks.) Which areas are best? What is better, furnished or unfurnished?

◆ Student lets. Do your student children have friends queuing up to share with them? Will their rents cover your mortgage payments? Check that your children's friends' parents are not all doing the same thing.

VOID PERIODS

Voids: a word to drive misery into the heart of any property investor. Void weeks or months are the periods between tenants when the property lies empty and you are receiving no income, but when you still have to pay the mortgage, insurance and bills, and at the same time keep the property secure, dry and habitable. It is far better to accept a slightly lower rent in order to attract good, reliable tenants who are in it for the long term. This is especially true in areas where there is already a good supply of rental properties.

Ideally, the moment a tenant gives notice you advertise for a new one and have them lined up and ready to move in once you have cleaned, carried out repairs and perhaps redecorated. But in practice it could take a while, especially if there are plenty of letting properties in your area and therefore plenty of choice for good tenants.

So plan when doing your initial calculations on income for at least one void month a year. (A month is about the length of an average void period.) Do not expect one set of tenants to leave on a Friday with the next lot moving in seamlessly on the following Monday. This will not happen. And remember that if your property sits empty for two months you are down more than 16% on your annual income.

YOUR VALUABLE TIME

The merits or otherwise of using agents will be discussed later in the book. For now though consider how involved you would *like* to be. Remember that you do not have to hand over the whole project to a third party: you can dip in and out, depending on your available time and relevant talents. So stages to think about for now are:

- finding a suitable property
- handling the purchase
- preparing and, if necessary, furnishing it for occupation
- finding the first tenants.

And after you have bought the property:

- managing the tenants or guests
- managing the inside of the property
- if it is a holiday let, the weekly cleaning
- looking after the garden and other exterior maintenance
- keeping the books.

You may have unlimited spare time and be happy to invest as many hours as it takes. But you will have to live near your rental property, probably within 30 miles or about an hour's drive, if you want to take on the routine maintenance, cleaning and gardening. When doing your sums you may want to take into account your time. If you have an existing job, use your salary expressed as an hourly rate as a basis for deciding if it is cost effective for you to devote hours to your property or whether it is better employing someone else to do it for you.

You also have to decide how valuable your free time is *to you*. If for example you already have a demanding job which leaves little time to devote to family and friends, do you really want to take on the extra responsibilities of routine maintenance or emergency call-outs for your property? Is it better to subcontract the work out to someone reliable and local?

Do not look upon using your own time as a financial saving because it is not. You should start thinking of your property as an investment, where everything comes at a price.

POTENTIAL DISASTERS

So you have thought about your reasons behind wanting to invest in a second property, done your sums and perhaps decided on your commitment level. At this point now look ahead and consider the worst that can happen, and what you can do in advance to protect yourself and your investment.

Nothing will ever give you guaranteed peace of mind and if you are fragile and nervous then this probably is not the business for you anyway. But there are ways of minimising the *chances* of something going wrong. Most but not all potential problems are insurable.

Problem	Avoidance/remedy
Structural	Full structural survey in advance
Subsidence	Adequate insurance, but expect excess of minimum £1,000
Fire, flood, storms, etc	Adequate insurance and good risk management
Contents damage	Adequate insurance, including accidental damage cover
Civil unrest/riot	Adequate insurance
Public liability	Specialist landlord insurance
Liability to employees	Specialist landlord insurance
Prevented from letting (because of insurable risk)	Specialist landlord insurance
Alternative accommodation	Specialist landlord insurance
Theft by tenant/guest	Specialist landlord insurance

Tenant rent default	Specialist landlord insurance
Legal disputes	Legal expenses insurance cover
Squatters	Specialist landlord insurance and correctly drawn up Tenancy Agreement
Void periods	Usually uninsurable
Foot and Mouth type incident	Partially insurable
Economic recession	Do not over borrow
Interest rate rises	Do not over borrow
Negative equity	Do not over borrow

Insurance is explored in more detail in Chapter 11.

CRYSTAL BALL GAZING

Finally, look ahead and consider what you *think* may happen in the particular sector of the housing market you are hoping to enter in the short, medium and long term. Unfortunately there is no magic formula, but try to imagine the wider picture.

- If you think a full-blown global recession is likely, are you prepared and able to sit it out?

- Do you expect (on the whole) an early return to the days of steadily rising property values?

- Are you super-confident and look forward to a return to the good old days of inflation-busting hyper growth?

- Are you confident there will be a regular supply of tenants or guests for your property, regardless of the general economic picture?

Some people are better informed than others but no one really knows what will happen. If you are generally pessimistic about the future of the property market then you are probably better off out of it. If on the other hand you are prepared and patient and generally upbeat then it is probably worth trying, but build an appropriate safety margin into your plans.

2

Raising the Money

RECENT HISTORY...

A decade or more ago this book probably would not have been written. There would have been little point because back then it was all but impossible to borrow money at a competitive rate to invest in something which you were not going to live in yourself.

Professional property developers had access to commercial loans while private individuals who found themselves having to let (because they were working abroad for example) were often only grudgingly allowed to do so by their lenders, and usually had to pay the price with higher interest rates and insurance premiums.

...AND WHAT CHANGED

The big change came in 1996 when Buy to Let mortgages were launched. Organisations like the Association of Residential Letting Agents (ARLA), with the backing of a panel of mortgage lenders, had realised that changes to the Housing Acts of 1988 and 1996 made letting a much more attractive option because rent controls and the risk of sitting tenants had been removed.

At about the same time it had begun to dawn on many lenders that they were stuck with lots of young and risky first-time buyers who had been attracted to the market prematurely by the housing boom of the late 1980s. In contrast, the borrowers who were expected to be attracted by Buy to Let mortgages would be older, financially more sophisticated and with capital behind them: in short, a far safer commercial bet. And so it turned out to be: arrears on properties bought with Buy to Let mortgages ran at about half what they were on properties bought with standard residential mortgages.

Interestingly, the introduction of these Buy to Let mortgages generated interest in the private rented sector, which had been in decline for a century, and helped make it respectable again. The seedy image of landlord Mr Rigsby, his sad tenant Miss Jones and *Rising Damp* had finally been banished.

These days of course there are other ways to finance the purchase of second properties, but the introduction of Buy to Let mortgages helped bring thousands of extra people into the market who would probably not have been able to do it in any other way.

WHEN TO GO FOR ADVICE

If you are an experienced, sophisticated investor with time on your hands, and your application is likely to be straightforward, you may well prefer to spend a few hours on the internet and phoning around before making up your own mind and filling out your own forms. After all, there is hardly a shortage of information out there. The problem is that there is far too much and it is time-consuming to sort out the good, reliable detail from the rubbish. So consider going through a mortgage broker or financial adviser if:

◆ You do not have the time or inclination to do your own research.
◆ You are not confident on the internet.
◆ You do not have easy broadband access to it.
◆ You are not confident about doing your own sums.
◆ You are not confident about interpreting the mass of figures and terms your internet research will throw up.

Remember too that brokers or financial advisers may be able to get discounts that you as an individual cannot. An intermediary such as a broker may also be useful if your borrowing requirements are not typical or straightforward. There are several reasons why this might be:

◆ The property you want to buy is non-standard (for example: unusual design or construction, ex-local authority, above commercial premises, in a block more than four stories high).
◆ You want to borrow beyond the usual financial limits.
◆ You may have a poor credit history.
◆ You may want to let to local authorities.
◆ You may want to let direct to local authority tenants.

- You may want to let to housing associations.
- You may want to deal only with the corporate market.
- You may be considering investing in Houses in Multiple Occupation (HMOs), for example, a house made up of bedsits.
- You may want to put the property in the name of a limited company.

Different mortgage companies favour different sorts of mortgage applications and you can waste a huge amount of time trying to identify which ones may be best for you, especially if any of the above points apply. So this is where a decent broker can start earning their fee by coming up with a list of lenders to approach first.

A good broker should also know how best to navigate the mortgage application system and have personal contacts with lending managers (ie the ones who make the decisions and not the people who answer the phones) who will judge you on your individual merits and not how you look on a standard application form. Again, all this can be a big time-saver.

WHERE TO GO FOR ADVICE

In general, it is probably best to start with long-established mortgage brokers or financial advisers. Common sense tells you that if someone has been offering broadly the same service in the same area for the last 20 or 30 years they are probably doing something right. If the broker or adviser comes via a personal recommendation, then so much the better. Be aware that since January 2005 regulations have become far tougher and, depending on what advice is being offered, agents and advisers have to be authorised by the Financial Services Authority. Always check first.

It is now common for many brokers or advisers, or the companies they work for, to have links of some sort to lenders and insurance companies, though in some cases these links may be buried and not immediately obvious. This is not necessarily a problem: what is important is that the broker or adviser can offer a range of mortgages which are relevant to you.

Which? (The Consumers' Association) recommended that if possible you pay an up-front fee for the advice on the grounds that somewhere down the line you will pay for it anyway, and at least with a fee it is obvious. A fee should also mean that you get a product that is right for you and not one which has been recommended because it comes with a big commission for the broker. The downside to paying a fee is that you may end up paying it even if the deal falls through. And the commission-only brokers and advisers will also argue that they do not get paid unless the job is done to the customer's satisfaction.

Either way, check on the adviser's previous relevant experience. On the whole, if they were selling replacement windows or sitting their GCSEs the week before it is not a good sign. So before you sign up with anyone, establish:

◆ How independent is the advice on offer, for example is the adviser or broker tied to any particular lender or lenders? If so, how many.
◆ How are they paid? Do they receive commission from the lender or do they take a fee from you, or a combination of both?
◆ How thoroughly trained are they?
◆ How long have they been in the job?

- How much experience do they have of the Buy to Let market?
- What can they offer that you cannot do or find out for yourself?

If you are pleased with the service the broker provides and he or she comes up with a suitable lender, then stick to them both like glue. If at any stage you want to expand your property empire, then you can go back to these same people, save yourself an enormous amount of legwork and possibly negotiate a better deal next time round.

But even if you do go through an intermediary or broker, the final call is always yours. If you are serious about investing in a second property and want to minimise your risks, you should have a view on the general health of the economy, the likely direction of interest rates, what is happening to property prices and an awareness of any changes in legislation which could affect you.

Information on all the above is everywhere you look, but the personal finance pages of the weekend broadsheet newspapers are as good a place as any to start. Read them regularly and you will soon start building up your own picture.

RAISING MONEY: THE OPTIONS

What sort of mortgage you get will depend on what you intend to do with your letting property.

If you want to long let, ie anything six months or over which will be covered by an Assured Shorthold Tenancy Agreement in England and Wales or a Short Assured Tenancy Agreement in Scotland, then your realistic options are:

- Buy to Let mortgage
- re-mortgaging your existing property
- using your own money.

If you want to holiday let, then your realistic choices are:

- commercial loan
- re-mortgaging your existing property
- using your own money.

Self-certified and self-declared mortgages, where applicants do not have to provide proof of income, are usually intended by the lenders to be used for the purchase of main homes and not to fund investment properties.

Buy to Let mortgages

Buy to Let mortgages are a popular way of raising money for investment properties. They are designed to be self-funding, ie the rent covers the mortgage, but you will still usually have to demonstrate that you and your partner, if it is a joint application, have a total income of at least £20,000–£25,000 a year.

A myth grew up around Buy to Let mortgages. The myth is that lenders will joyfully let you borrow *more* than the value of the property, and once in possession of one of these fabulous mortgages, you just sit back and wait for the money to roll in.

In reality, it is not easy to fulfil all the conditions of a Buy to Let mortgage, and lenders are sometimes cautious when dealing with novices in this highly competitive market.

If you already have a portfolio of rental properties with a good earnings track record and a set of decent-looking books, then the lenders' attitude will be different and you may well be able to negotiate your own deals (and in that case you probably will not be reading this book). Otherwise:

◆ you will generally only be able to borrow an absolute maximum of 85% of the value of the property (loan-to-value, abbreviated to LTV)

◆ you will have to find the deposit from your own resources, (ie not borrow the money) and be able to prove that you can

◆ interest rates may not be as competitive as for domestic mortgages

◆ you will probably have to show that the rent will exceed the mortgage.

By far the most important condition of a Buy to Let mortgage is the last point, above, because if you cannot meet that condition then you will probably not be able to borrow the money. All lenders will expect that the monthly rent is at least sufficient to cover the monthly mortgage payment. In practice many lenders will expect a lot more: monthly rent equivalent to 125% of the monthly mortgage payment is about average, but some lenders will ask for as much as 150%.

It may not sound much, but the size of the margin will make a huge difference to your calculations. For example, if your monthly mortgage payment is £500 then this is the impact that different margins could have:

Margin	Rent you will have to charge*
100%	£500 per month
125%	£625 per month
150%	£750 per month

*The rent has to be confirmed by the valuer your mortgage company will instruct.

If you think there could be a gap between what the valuer may decide and the rent you need, it may be worth getting an opinion in advance from a letting agent. Their estimate of the rentable value may well be higher than that of the mortgage company, and if necessary it could help you negotiate the figure upwards.

There are good reasons why lenders usually expect the rent to exceed the mortgage by such a large amount.

◆ It means that if interest rates rise the rent you receive should still be enough to cover your higher mortgage payments.

◆ It allows for periods when the property is empty and earning no rent, but when the mortgage and insurances still have to be paid.

◆ It allows for periods when the property is empty and earning no rent, but when the utilities and repair and maintenance bills still have to paid.

Because the rent-to-mortgage ratio can restrict how much you can borrow, it will also determine the size of deposit you have to put down. Just because a mortgage company offers loans of up to 85% it will not do so *unless you can show the rent will exceed the mortgage by the required amount.*

The sums can be baffling. It may help to compare two examples to demonstrate how important the ratio or margin is, and to show how you may have to find a much larger deposit than you imagine.

Assume the purchase price of the property is £150,000, and you are applying for an interest-only mortgage at 5%. Your lender is asking that the rent is 125% of the mortgage.

Anticipated rent from the property:	£500
Monthly mortgage payment:	£400
(£400 × 125%)	
Which is the equivalent to a total mortgage of:	£96,000
(£96,000 × 5% p.a. ÷ 12 months)	
Leaving you to find a deposit of:	£54,000
Resulting in a LTV of:	64%

The above example means you have to put down a deposit of 36% of the purchase price, *but* you only have enough money for a deposit of 15%. The figures now look as shown below. (The purchase price, interest rate and rent/mortgage ratio of 125% stay the same.)

Deposit of 15% of the total purchase price:	£22,500
This means you need a mortgage of:	£127,500
Giving you a monthly mortgage payment of:	£531
(127,500 × 5% p.a. ÷ 12 months)	
Therefore the rent you have to charge will be:	£664
(£531 × 125%)	

But will the same property fetch £664 per month rent rather than the £500 you had originally expected? And, unfortunately, the sums can look even worse, depending on the interest rate the lender uses to calculate the mortgage rate. Some use the Standard Variable Rate (SVR) and a few assume a higher rate still. The effect this has is to increase the monthly mortgage payment which means the rent must rise accordingly.

What all this means in practice is that you may well have to find a larger deposit than you had originally anticipated or buy a cheaper property. Ideally what you need is a property which is cheap to buy but which commands a relatively high rent. As a general rule, a two-bedroomed property will be proportionately more profitable than a three-bedroomed property, but this is an extremely general rule and is dependent on area, the type of market you are going into, the levels of supply at the time, and property prices.

Remortgaging your existing property

If you have a small mortgage or even no mortgage at all on your family home this could be a cheaper and easier way of raising money than going down the Buy to Let route. Another advantage of remortgaging is that you can use the money for any legal purpose. This is especially useful if you do want to go into holiday letting because your borrowing options there are more limited.

As a general rule, you can remortgage your home for up to 85 or 90% of its value, as long as your income is enough to cover the loan. Any anticipated future income from the property you are buying cannot be taken into account at this stage. Like any remortgage, there will be some extra costs, for example survey, arrangement and valuation fees, but these will be small in proportion to your total investment in your letting property.

Remortgaging your existing property and chasing the best interest rate deals are hugely popular. Serial remortgagers are known in the industry as 'remortgage tarts'. If you are one of the majority who cannot be bothered to switch away from the Standard Variable Rate, you are an 'inert'. Which one are you?

Your own resources

Some people may be able to fund their investment in a second property themselves – perhaps after inheriting money, after the sale of a larger property which has freed up capital, buying with someone else (for example a sibling, parent, other relative or friend) or from some other windfall.

There are advantages and disadvantages to using your own money:

♦ Using your own money to invest in property provides some peace of mind because it removes the worry of interest rate rises...

♦ ...but will you worry *more* because it is your own money if property prices go down?

♦ If you do not have a mortgage then there is no interest to pay.

♦ There are no valuation or arrangement fees to pay and no lenders to be answerable to.

♦ But will you need the money for something else, school fees, early retirement or even to fund a deposit on a third property?

◆ Where will your money work hardest for you?

And are there any circumstances where it may be worth borrowing anyway?

◆ Will extra money buy a more expensive property which could eventually rise in value proportionately and bring in a greater income?

◆ Many businesses borrow to expand even if they have capital available: in the right circumstances it is accepted good business practice.

◆ Remember too that any interest you pay on your mortgage is a business expense and will ultimately help boost your profits by reducing your tax bill.

Commercial loans

If you want to buy a property and holiday let it from the start, and none of the above options apply to you, then you may have to consider a commercial loan. It is not great news because they are relatively expensive.

Both banks and building societies offer commercial loans. But they do not come cheap, especially when compared with the reasonable terms offered in the domestic mortgage market. A commercial loan will cost you $1-1\frac{1}{2}\%$ of the total borrowing just to arrange. Solicitors' costs are more expensive, then on top of that there are the standard survey, searches, etc, to pay for. Expect also:

- ◆ To pay a higher interest rate. There are no advertised rates as such, but they will usually be in the region of 2¼–2½% above the base rate.

- ◆ To put down a significant deposit. Depending on the area, it will be at least 30% and possibly as much as 40% of the purchase price.

- ◆ A shorter mortgage term. The usual limit is about ten or fifteen years, depending on the applicant's age.

- ◆ To take out a repayment mortgage. Interest-only commercial loans are rare.

TYPE OF MORTGAGE

This book is not a mortgage guide, so if you do not know the difference between trackers, fixed rates, discounts, caps, variables, etc, seek specialist advice. If after doing that you are none the wiser and are about to stick a pin in a list, then go for trackers linked to something like the Bank of England base rate because they will probably provide the fewest nasty surprises.

Repayment versus interest-only loans

Investors in second properties often elect for interest-only mortgages, ie the monthly payments only cover the interest on the loan and no attempt is made to pay back the capital. This is because many investors have no intention of keeping the property for a typical 25-year mortgage term: instead they will sell when the market is right (the average is between five and ten years), relying on the property increasing in value to pay off the loan and make them some money. In the meantime they have enjoyed extra income because interest-only mortgage payments are lower. This is fine in a rising market, but be prepared to hold onto your investment property over the longer term if prices remain depressed.

If you are naturally more cautious and do not take to the idea of having a huge loan for a long period which never goes down, then a straight repayment mortgage may be best for you. But do remember that your monthly costs will be much higher and the rent may not cover the mortgage. Also remember that inflation does gradually eat into the borrowings and after five or ten years it probably won't seem anything like as alarming.

As far as stock market-linked investments are concerned, fairly or not, endowments have been largely discredited. There are many other market-linked investments designed to produce growth over the long term in order to pay back a mortgage, but again they may not be for the faint-hearted or overly cautious.

WHAT LENDERS WILL WANT FROM YOU

◆ Whatever the circumstances, you will almost always have to demonstrate you have enough resources to cover the initial deposit. A possible exception would be if you are considering investing in an off-plan property (where it has not actually been built yet) and the developer or agent is keen to offer incentives to prospective buyers.

◆ An assurance that the property will be fit to let within two to four weeks of the completion date.

◆ If you are investing in property for long lets, then the lender will probably want to see a copy of the Tenancy Agreement you intend using.

◆ A check on your age. Your age on the date the mortgage is due to end is not as critical as it used to be. With some Buy to Let mortgages the limit is 75, but on others there is no age limit at all. For other mortgages or loans, the lender will usually expect you to be no older than 65 or 70 years old when the term expires.

◆ With Buy to Let the lenders' checklist will go in something like this order:
  – establish income of at least £20,000–£25,000 p.a.
  – confirm proof of identity and address
  – pass credit checks
  – surveyor confirms property value and likely letting income.

DO NOT BORROW MORE THAN YOU CAN AFFORD

Everything in this chapter has been written on the rather obvious assumption that you are planning to tell the truth to potential lenders about your income, circumstances and intentions.

It is probably easier now than it has ever been to get in too deep. Firstly, the mortgage system is more flexible than it used to be, fewer questions are asked and fewer checks made. Secondly, there is fierce competition among lenders, brokers and other intermediaries and some will help you bend the system in order to secure your business (and therefore their fee or commission). But remember that it is still your signature on the dotted line and your legal responsibility to make sure the information you give is correct.

Do not think that if a lender is prepared to turn a blind eye to some of your figures and advance you X amount, then it must be OK. Remember that this is not the same as a mortgage on the family home where lenders may be sympathetic if you run into problems. Investing in a second property is a commercial proposition: it is fine if you keep up with the payments but do not expect much leniency or mercy if you cannot.

There are two standard questions to check you are not over-borrowing:

♦ If interest rates shoot up 2% tomorrow can you cope comfortably with the higher mortgage payments?

♦ If the property is empty for three months can you afford the mortgage payments?

DO NOT GET TOO HUNG UP ON MORTGAGES

After saying all that, the irony in raising finance and selecting a mortgage is that it is one of the lesser decisions you will have to make as an investor in the second homes' market. Yes, your monthly repayments will be affected and you may not be able to repay chunks of capital in the early years without penalty, but all this is marginal compared to the big picture:

♦ Should you be investing in a second property at all?
♦ When should you be doing it?
♦ Where and what should you buy?
♦ Who will your tenants or guests be?
♦ How well should you maintain your property?
♦ When should you sell it?

Unless you have second sight and direct access to the Bank of England Monetary Policy Committee (the important people who set interest rates), you will never successfully judge exactly the right product for you, on exactly the right terms, at the right time and from the right lender. A third of one per cent on your mortgage rate here, a free valuation there, a £500 cashback somewhere else: all this will mean relatively little over the typical life of a mortgage. So don't waste time on the finer detail if it means you lose sight of the overview.

3

The Right Property

There is one important rule in this chapter. *Do not buy a property because you like it: buy it because it is suitable for its intended purpose.*

Blindingly obvious perhaps, but a remarkable number of people are swayed by nice views or a big kitchen. This approach is no good at all. Property may be more subjective than shares, bonds or building society accounts, but you still need to reach your decision in an analytical and calculating way. Personal taste or preference should not come into it.

By now you should have a fairly good idea of what you want from your property and how much you can afford to spend. So at this point, and before you go looking, draw up a list of the *must haves* you are looking for in your investment property.

Some questions to think about:

LONG LETS
◆ Maximum price.
◆ House or flat.
◆ New or old.
◆ Purpose built or conversion.
◆ Large or small rooms.
◆ Does it need its own entrance?
◆ Does it need a garden?
◆ Does it need its own parking?
◆ Freehold or leasehold.
◆ Minimum number of bedrooms.
◆ Minimum number of bathrooms.
◆ Separate kitchen and reception room, or combined.
◆ Close to shops.
◆ Close to entertainments.
◆ Close to public transport.
◆ Close to good road links.
◆ Close to good schools.
◆ Close to business centres.
◆ Close to large businesses and/or organisations.

HOLIDAY LETS
◆ Maximum price.
◆ Cottage or apartment.
◆ New or old.
◆ Chocolate box or functional.
◆ Rural, village, town, city or coastal.

- Minimum number of bedrooms
- Minimum number of bathrooms
- Separate kitchen and reception room, or combined.
- Views.
- Easily accessible.
- Quiet.
- Large or small garden.
- Swimming pool.
- How much parking?
- Close to shops.
- Close to entertainments.
- Close to beaches.
- Close to moors or mountains.

You should end up with a list of features your investment property must have, may have and certainly does not want. The list will be useful if you intend to look for the property yourself or employ an agent to do it for you.

THE IMPORTANCE OF RESEARCH...

Even if you already have a detailed knowledge of the area where you are considering buying, or intend to employ a relocation or search agent, it is still safest to do some research, if only to check the current situation. This will help you find out:

- How buoyant or depressed the local market is.
- What prices are doing.
- What is a fair price for the type of properties you are interested in.
- If there is an over or under-supply of any types of property.
- How long properties are taking to sell.
- Which type of properties come up again and again.

- Which properties are difficult to shift.
- Which areas are sought after.
- Which areas are up and coming.
- Which areas are suspiciously cheap (and why).

That will give you the broad picture, but micro-detail is necessary too, so find out:

- Why do houses in village A take longer to sell than in neighbouring village B?

- Flats in development C are expensive but go quickly. What have they got that flats in development D do not have?

- One row of fabulous Georgian townhouses backs onto light industrial units: the townhouses on the other side of the street have a pretty canal at the bottom of their gardens. What is the price difference?

And so on. There is an argument that this level of homework is not really necessary. After all, you get a general feel for the area, find a decent agent and then sit back while he or she does the legwork. This is true, but at the same time everything you find out, no matter how insignificant, helps minimise risk and maximise profit.

...AND HOW TO DO IT

The internet
This is the place to start for an overview, especially if you live away from your targeted area. It is a good research tool but interestingly, even though it is now well-established and virtually everyone has access to it, it is still largely used for preliminary

research. Very few property sales are conducted and concluded online.

There are scores of ever-changing property sites around, but three of the largest and most comprehensive are:

◆ www.ukpropertyshop.co.uk
◆ www.rightmove.co.uk
◆ www.primelocation.co.uk

Sites like these provide details of thousands of properties across the country and they give you a good general feel for what is available and how much it is likely to cost. The sites, along with many others, also offer search facilities which allows you to narrow down your requests: for example, a three-bedroom, two-bathroom period cottage in the Peak District, with the minimum and maximum price you are prepared to pay.

Rightmove leans towards the domestic residential market, so if you are considering long letting this would be a good place to start. Primelocation is slightly more general, so the choice of potential holiday letting properties may be wider. Propertyshop has an excellent list of local estate agents.

Sites like these are updated frequently but others may not be as conscientious, so before you get fired up about a property call the selling agent and check it is still available.

Local newspapers
These are an invaluable source of detailed information. In most areas there are usually one or two local newspapers which publish

sizeable weekly property supplements. If you live away, take out a subscription and get them sent to you. As well as the properties, pay attention to the estate agents who sell them. Agents say they will sell anything, but in practice most specialise. Consider which ones seem to deal mainly in the sort of properties you are interested in. There is not much point getting on the mailing list of an agent who sells estate starter homes if you are hoping to go into luxury holiday cottages.

Estate agents

You now have a list of relevant estate agents. Phone them, get them interested in you, make it clear you are looking for an investment property, tell them your price range and give them a copy of your must-have list. Ask their advice. Find out what is around and how realistic your expectations are.

House price surveys

These are heavily — some would say – over-reported. The surveys probably say as much about the general economic health of the country as they do about the realities of what is happening to house prices in specific areas.

Remember that many house price surveys *only monitor prices of properties which are being bought with mortgages.* In holiday areas, where second homes and holiday cottages are common, a lot of properties are bought for cash. Therefore they never feature in these surveys and it follows that the surveys cannot accurately reflect what is happening in those areas.

In theory, the Land Registry survey should be the most accurate because it reflects the price that *the property actually fetched,* whether it was bought for cash or via a mortgage. However it is an average, and like any average it can be distorted by one or two exceptionally low or exceptionally high prices in an area of few sales.

But do not ignore the house price surveys. Read them all and then use them to help create a big picture of the housing market, rather than basing your entire investment strategy around them.

Word of mouth

Word of mouth can also help contribute to the big picture, but it is not the method for accumulating detailed and accurate market research. Where word of mouth is invaluable is in building up a general impression of local feeling, especially on a specific issue. Is that village likely to get its new bypass? What do people really think about the vast new supermarket/porn shop/prison which has just opened down the road?

WHO LOOKS FOR THE PROPERTY

There are three basic choices:

◆ You do the looking yourself. This is fine if you already live in the area and have some spare time, but not so easy if you live away or are busy with family or work commitments.

◆ You retain an independent relocation or search agent on your behalf. They will do the research, view properties and negotiate the price. Some charge an initial registration fee of a few hundred pounds, some charge one or two per cent of the eventual purchase price and some charge a combination of the two. In any event, most have a minimum fee of around £1,000–£1,500.

- You instruct an estate agent to act for you (you are known as a retained client). Again they put in the legwork, drawing on their own list of properties and local contacts and will also speak to other estate agents who may have suitable properties. In this case the estate agent you instruct is acting for you as buyer, and not the seller, and therefore you pay them. A typical fee would be around 2% of the purchase price.

WHERE TO BUY

Long letting

If you are considering long lets then you have many more geographic options. Decent properties on a long let will always attract tenants, with the following provisos:

- Unless you are hoping to attract benefit-supported tenants or enter into a partnership with a housing association, look for an economically sound area with continuing good prospects and low unemployment.

- Do not go into an area which already has a glut of rental properties. The ready availability of Buy to Let mortgages has meant increasingly that in some areas there is now over-supply which has driven rents down.

- If you are looking at flats, check there is an active management company. Some mortgage companies will not be happy lending without one (because there is no single person or group to take responsibility for communal and outside areas).

- Look closely at typical rents in the area you are considering in relation to property prices. Forget any area which has high purchase prices and low rents which mean poor yields. This is especially true in times of depressed or flat property markets when you cannot depend on increases in capital values.

◆ Do not take on anything too unusual or not in keeping with the area because you will restrict the potential number of tenants who may be interested. A gothic, open-plan church conversion with one huge room and 25-foot high ceilings in a suburban area dominated by family homes is not going to have the number of potential takers as the same property in an urban area where singles and couples are more common.

Holiday letting

Unless there are excellent reasons otherwise, only consider areas where there is an established visitor market. You may personally appreciate pockets of a former coalfield region or the Midlands manufacturing belt, and be tempted by the cheaper prices, but the critical mass of potential guests you are going to need will be looking elsewhere. So consider:

◆ The National Parks, including the Brecon Beacons or Snowdonia in Wales; the Cairngorms in Scotland; or the Lakes, Dartmoor or the Yorkshire Dales in England.

◆ Established English holiday areas, for example Devon and Cornwall, Norfolk, the Isle of Wight and the Cotswolds.

◆ The prettier English shires like Shropshire and Hampshire.

◆ The Gower Peninsula and Pembrokeshire in Wales.

◆ The Highlands, the more accessible islands, the Southern Uplands, and Dumfries and Galloway in Scotland.

- In Northern Ireland, County Antrim's Causeway Coast, Strangford Lough or the Mourne Mountains.

Also think about towns and cities with strong historical and/or cultural attraction which already attract many visitors, for example:

- London
- Bath
- York
- Oxford
- Cambridge
- Edinburgh.

And don't forget areas which are benefiting from the huge growth in activity holidays, for example where cycle routes or long-distance paths have opened in the last few years.

The above suggestions are by no means exhaustive, but at least will provide you with ideas and a starting point. In practice your choice may well be dictated by existing family ties, personal preference, access from your home and your budget.

WHAT TO BUY

Long letting

Unfortunately there is not much romance in the type of property which makes a good long letting proposition. If you want to maximise your chances of letting by appealing to the largest possible number of potential tenants, then it is safest to go for something middle-of-the-road. That means:

- something less than 20 years old, properly constructed and easily mortgageable
- in a town or city
- with good central heating
- with a garden
- no carpets in the kitchen or bathroom
- ceramic tiles in the kitchen (white goods constantly moved in and out rip lino)
- steel and not plastic baths (they are practically the same price)
- with showers as well as baths
- satellite or cable TV connection
- broadband connection
- off-road parking, preferably with a garage, especially in towns.

If you are going for the family market, then consider that most families with children prefer properties with manageable gardens. (Note *manageable*: it is reasonable to expect tenants to mow a medium-sized lawn and weed a couple of flower beds: it is quite another for them to take on something the size of Kew Gardens.) Ideally, the property will have its own entrance, with space for a push chair/buggy. If there are three or more bedrooms, then many tenants will expect at least one en suite bathroom as well as a family bathroom. The kitchen should ideally be large enough to eat in and suitable to be described as a 'family room', ie there is also space for a TV, PC, sofa and a few toys. Lots of cupboards and storage spaces are essential. Outside space for keeping bicycles is also useful.

If your target tenants are more likely to be non-family, ie childless, then outside space, storage space and larger family rooms are not so important. What they will expect instead is a higher proportion of bathrooms to bedrooms (especially at the top end of the market) and a well-fitted kitchen, with high quality white goods and space for lots of gadgets.

Holiday letting

After location, above all, when considering what to buy, remember that holiday cottages have to be thoroughly cleaned in a short space of time, week after week, month after month, so avoid anything too fiddly or ornate. Exposed beams, inglenooks and ancient panelling in old properties look great in brochures, but are a nightmare to keep clean. Beams and rafters only create more angles for spiders to spin their webs, while dust and dead flies collect in and on anything which is not a flat and smooth vertical surface. Obviously, unless you are deliberately aiming for the urban minimalist look, square box-like rooms do not look inviting. So, when you view a property, imagine how easy it will be to keep clean, and try to strike a balance between easy maintenance, comfort and atmosphere.

Think too about the layout. Properties which have a separate bedroom and en suite bathroom, and even a small living area, perhaps on its own floor or in an annexe, are popular because of the privacy they provide. They go down particularly well with families who holiday with grandparents or noisy teenagers, where both sides may want to keep their distance.

A suite of rooms on the ground floor is also useful for any guests who may have problems tackling flights of steep cottage stairs. But make sure any separate set of rooms is not too isolated: if the parties wanted that much privacy they probably would not be going on holiday together in the first place.

Depending on which area of the market you are going for, you may also want to think about properties with swimming pools. They can be a huge draw, especially in properties some way from the sea, but you will need to think carefully about children and safety.

INHERITING PROPERTY

Significant numbers of people now inherit property and, perhaps for sentimental reasons, do not want to sell and so decide to rent it out. However, all the same rules still apply: is it right for its purpose? Are the kitchen and bathroom sufficiently modern? Does it have parking?

It may not be an easy decision to make, but you may be better off selling an inherited property and using the money to buy something more appropriate.

PROS AND CONS OF BUYING AN EXISTING RENTAL PROPERTY

On the whole it is probably easiest and safest to buy a property with vacant possession, ie it is empty.

However, if you find your dream property and it already has a tenant, then this is not necessarily a disaster. Assuming the tenant has signed the standard Tenancy Agreement, then you simply take over that contract from the vendor and your interests are protected in the same way as they would have been had you signed the original agreement.

If, however, the property contains a tenant who enjoys any sort of protected tenancy then seek professional legal advice. It may be easier to find another property to buy.

If you are considering buying a property which is holiday let for the foreseeable future, this may be simpler legally but more complicated logistically. Usually in this instance you would agree to take over the contract, if there is one, which exists between the vendor and their letting agency, and honour any future bookings. The problem occurs, especially if the property is heavily booked, when it comes to moving furniture. Obviously you cannot move one set of furniture out and another set in, as well as make good any damage and clean, in a few hours on changeover day. So you either wait for a lengthy gap between bookings or you negotiate to buy the vendor's furniture.

CITY DEVELOPMENTS AND LOFT LIVING

City developments justify their own mini-section because the lettings climate is very different from what you may experience elsewhere.

There is now hardly a town or city left in the country which has not seen some sort of redevelopment of its old warehouses and other industrial sites. In some areas, notably central London, there has been serious over-supply, and prices – and sometimes the quality of build – have fallen. In northern cities like Manchester, Liverpool and Leeds, hundreds are languishing on the market and there are many more still being built.

Many so-called lofts were bought by investors, attracted by high rents and still rising property prices, using the inevitable Buy to Let mortgages. This has led to some developments, especially in London, being up to 90% let to tenants. This is not necessarily bad, but it can result in a rather soulless atmosphere, more like a hotel, where communal inside areas and gardens may not be particularly well maintained. Realistically, not even the best-run management company is going to take as much loving care of a building as its fond owners.

Also consider that in some areas, investors have been buying and selling these inner city apartments off-plan (before they have been built) as if they were commodities, in other words as a tradeable asset rather than as a place to live. This means the prices are being pushed up for all the wrong reasons. It is fine if the investors are still there: but when prices peak (as they have in plenty of areas) and the speculators' attentions turn elsewhere, will there still be enough people around who want to rent your property and live in it? There is also concern over the sustainability and social cost of these developments, because families and the elderly have been squeezed out by the urban professional.

If, while reading this, you still think it is a good idea to buy and sell these apartments quickly yourself, and perhaps make some easy money, then think again. If you have not done so already, then you are probably far too late. If, however, you are determined, then at least speak to local independent letting and estate agents beforehand. They will be able to advise you which are the obvious white elephants and which units are in greater demand.

But house conversions or developments where less than 20% of the units are rented out are probably a safer bet. Ultimately, the more owner-occupiers there are, the better looked after the building will probably be, and therefore more attractive to future tenants and future buyers.

HOW TO BUY YOUR PROPERTY

Not as daft as it sounds because estate agents, and Solicitors' Property Centres in Scotland, are not the only option. The alternatives include:

Auctions

Auctions are not for the faint-hearted. If your bid has been successful, the moment the auctioneer's hammer drops, it is legally yours and no excuses. The hammer dropping is the equivalent of exchange of contracts on a standard property transaction and it does not matter that you will not have signed anything. You should have conducted your survey, searches and other legal checks before sale day, so if you do not succeed in your bid then you will have wasted your money. On the day of the sale you have to pay a 10% deposit and the balance is usually due between 21 and 28 days later.

There is myth surrounding auctions (a bit like those myths on fabulous Buy to Let mortgages). The myth here is that it is possible to pick up the most astonishing bargains at auctions. (Amazing: no one else has ever thought of it – not even professional speculators?) That may well have been the case years ago, but not any more.

Many of the properties which come up at auction could be derelict or all but. This is because they can be difficult to price accurately, especially if they are sitting on a good plot. But often, anything decent and habitable will have already been sold in the usual way.

Occasionally, unusual properties (either location or design) are sold at auctions because again it is not easy to put an accurate value on them. Remember though that if you do go for one of these, just make sure it is not so unusual that it is difficult to let (water tower, no windows).

Auctions are fine if you are confident and have done your homework first. If you are seriously considering buying at auction, then go along to one or two first to get a feel for how they work. Also have a look at a good auction information site, www.eigroup.co.uk. And remember the golden rule: *never* go over your predetermined limit. If you are worried about your self-control, take along a friend who can be relied upon to keep their head and drag you out if things look like they are getting out of hand.

Buying privately online
Despite the internet, which promised to revolutionise property sales by banishing estate agents into the abyss for ever, buying and selling online has still not really caught on in a big way. Do not rule it out, look by all means: just do not count on it.

Buying privately elsewhere
Try *word of mouth*. Tell the world what you are after, family, friends, acquaintances, business contacts, anyone, and wait and see what happens. Many really good properties never come on the market because they are snapped up privately first.

Leafleting can be particularly effective (and cheap) if you have identified a street or small area where you would like to buy your investment property. There are between one and a quarter and one and a half million property transactions each year, plus many others who are thinking about it, so statistically you should stumble upon someone who should at least consider an offer.

Make sure the leaflet is professional and printed to show you are serious. Make it clear if you are not in a chain, which can be a huge advantage. If you are a cash buyer this is even better, so say so. If you are really desperate/interested in a property, consider offering an up-front deposit of, say, £5,000–£10,000. But only do this after speaking to your solicitor who can arrange the paperwork accordingly.

Try *newspaper adverts*. Find the local newspapers which publish property supplements. Look at the adverts and decide which stands out and why. Something boxed and with lots of white space around the words is usually best. Write your advert, keep it short, and again stress if you are chain-free, a cash buyer or able to move quickly.

SEARCHES

Once you have found a possible property, pay particular attention to the results of searches your solicitor will conduct on your behalf. Remember that if a problem emerges on what would be your family home you can decide if you can live with it: tenants or guests may not be so accommodating and can easily go elsewhere, especially if there is plenty of choice.

Local authority searches should throw up anything they control. This could be proposed new roads or new housing planned for your immediate area. They should also reveal if there are any current planning consents granted for your property.

Environmental searches are increasingly common, especially on former brownfield sites where there may be concerns over the previous use of the land.

Mining checks may also be necessary in some areas which have been heavily worked in the past in order to establish where the old workings are.

SURVEYS

As with searches, remember that if a problem emerges when you and your family are living in the property, you will just have to put up with builders, plumbers or electricians, but your guest or tenant can walk away. So think about commissioning a more thorough survey than you usually would. There are three choices:

1. *Valuation.* The mortgage company instructs a surveyor to confirm that there is a property standing, that it is a suitable lending risk, and that it would fetch X on the market. The mortgage company's main concern is that if you default they can recoup their money. By no stretch of the imagination is this a survey.

2. *Home buyers' report.* The surveyor will inspect the visible parts of the property and tell you if there is any obvious problem, sign of collapse, rot, infestation, and so on, but he or she will probably not lift carpets or move large furniture.

3. *Full structural survey.* This will probably tell you far more than you ever need know (or understand), but you may want to be particularly cautious and go for this option, especially if the property is old.

NEIGHBOURS

At about this stage, take a long hard look at the neighbours. Any existing serious problems or disputes should have been disclosed by the vendor, but it still does pay to do your own homework. A bit of extra work now could save much hassle in the future. As an owner-occupier, you can decide to live with a problem: tenants or guests don't have to.

◆ If families are likely to be your tenants, are there students nearby?

◆ Where are the elderly?

◆ Where are the noisy and/or dangerous dogs?

◆ Are the walls and floors substantial enough to block out most of the noise from neighbours?

◆ Are there any joint hedges or communal areas which may be a potential problem?

◆ Is parking clearly demarcated?

Be fussy when looking for your investment property. Take as long as you need. This is not a family home where there may be pressure to buy quickly because you have already sold and there are the children's schools to worry about. So wait and keep waiting until you have found the perfect, hassle-free letting property, and you are as sure as you can be.

4

Who Needs an Agent Anyway?

The big advantage of using an agency is that they do the dirty work for you. They act as a buffer between you and a problem tenant or guest, chase up missing money, or if it comes to the worst, help evict them. But of course everything comes at a price, and it is up to you to decide if it is a price worth paying.

It is important at this stage to distinguish between letting agents who find you long-term tenants and the holiday letting companies who find you guests for your holiday cottage. The first is literally your agent, acting on your behalf and with certain legal delegated powers. The second is effectively a marketing organisation which promotes and sells time in your cottage to a third party.

WHAT LONG-LETTINGS AGENCIES DO

Most agencies offer two separate services. The first is finding you a tenant (often called the 'front end'), and the second is managing the tenancy once it is under way. You can usually ask the agent to do both or one or the other.

Finding the tenant

Agents will:

* Advise on the rental value of your property.
* Advise you on costs and expenses.
* Market your property through newspaper and magazine adverts, the internet or estate agents, where appropriate.
* Arrange viewings by prospective tenants (agents should ideally accompany them: a decent agent can tell a lot about a prospective tenant by meeting them personally).
* Select a suitable tenant.
* Take up the tenant's references, usually from their former landlord, bank and employer, and sometimes a personal reference. (NB: Landlords should ask to see these references: it is a check to make sure the agent has done them.)
* Make credit checks.
* Draw up the inventory and report on the property's condition.
* Arrange the Tenancy Agreement between the tenant and yourself.
* Collect the tenant's deposit.
* Arrange standing orders for the transfer of the rent.
* See the tenant into the property, arranging for the handover of keys and ensuring a smooth transfer.
* Contact the utilities and give them the name and moving in date of the new tenant.

They do not have to do everything on the list, but the more checks that are carried out and the more thorough the preparation and thought that goes into a tenancy initially, the less likely it is to go wrong. Remember that an extra day's work now, a few more phone calls or emails and a couple of hundred pounds to the agent, could save much time, hassle and money later on.

Managing a tenancy once it is underway
Agents will:

- Arrange for repairs.
- Arrange for regular servicing and maintenance of appliances and burglar alarms.
- Arrange rent collection.
- Regularly inspect the property (usually quarterly).
- Liaise between the tenant and yourself.

At the end of the tenancy
Agents will:

- See the tenant out of the property.
- Take back the keys.
- Check the inventory and the condition of the property and negotiate any deductions from the deposit to cover breakages and damage.
- Return what is left of the deposit.
- Tell the utilities that the tenant has left.

Some agents will not agree to manage your property if they have not selected the tenant in the first place, so you may have to shop around if you want to do it that way. In practice though there is probably little point: finding a decent tenant is what takes the time, and if that is done properly then the subsequent management should be quite painless.

HOW TO FIND A DECENT AGENT

This is the Holy Grail. It is critical to find a responsible agent to manage your property, especially if you live some distance away or are unable to keep an eye on it for any other reason. You have to trust them and have faith in their judgement. If you get a poor agent, it could mean anything from allowing rent arrears to build up, to failing to monitor the condition of the property, or not organising the regular servicing of appliances.

It is not easy to find a good agent. By far the best method is word-of-mouth recommendation from someone whose opinions you trust. Otherwise:

♦ Look in local newspapers and check the letting agents' adverts. Whose adverts are professionally presented? Who is renting properties which are similar to yours? Who has a brisk turnover of properties?

♦ Give the agents a ring and trust your instincts. Do they sound professional? Authoritative? Keen for your business?

♦ Ask them if they maintain a separate account for client's money.

♦ Check that they carry professional indemnity insurance.

♦ Ask for references from other landlords who are currently with the agent.

◆ Invite around to your letting property the two or three agents who have most impressed you on the phone. Ask for their impressions and their assessment of what the rent should be.

AGENCY CHARGES
Fees will vary wildly depending on where you are in the country.

Many charge a flat fee (usually with VAT on top) for a 'tenant find'. This could be a couple of hundred pounds or more. Other agents charge the equivalent of half a month's rent, or even one month, depending on how much work is involved. Some agents charge extra for taking up references, compiling inventories (especially if they are detailed), making credit checks, and so on.

If you retain the agent (or find another one) to manage the property on a continuing basis, expect to pay them about 10–15% of each month's rent, plus VAT. Some agents will charge slightly more (perhaps another two or three per cent) if the owner lives abroad because it means the agents will carry extra responsibility for managing the property. Some letting agents' fees in central London and other large cities may be higher, possibly closer to 17–18% of the monthly rent plus VAT.

You may be able to negotiate a reduction in fees, especially if you have more than one letting property. Otherwise it will depend on local conditions and how hungry the agent is for your business. If there is a glut of letting properties in the area, and agents are rushed off their feet, then forget it.

SHOULD YOU GO IT ALONE?
Generally you need an agent if you live some way away (anything over about 40 miles or an hour or so in the car), if you do not

have the time or inclination to do it yourself, or if you are nervous and likely to be wobbly if the tenant refuses to pay the rent or move out.

Finding the tenant and carrying out the initial checks

Only consider doing this yourself if you live locally, know the area well, and really do have the time and the stamina to carry out all the checks. Also, while you are weighing up your options, keep reminding yourself that good letting agents know how and where to find decent tenants, and really good agents can spot the potential tenants from hell a mile off.

If you decide to find your own tenant, carry out all the basic checks first to establish their identity, their previous address and where they work, by taking up the references you should have asked for. You may also want to carry out some further checks, and there are some good internet sites to help you do this.

Experian runs a well-organised and clear site, www.tenantverifier. com. For about £10 you get a basic check on a prospective tenant, about £20 gets you slightly more detail, and there is a more expensive annual subscription if you think that you may be using the site a lot. Another good, well-laid out and comprehensive site is www.homeletuk.com which offers tenant checks, along with landlord's insurance, details on Buy to Let mortgages, removals and storage.

Another site – www.192.com – helps you to establish if people and companies are where they say they are (useful in checking out referees). This is a subscription service, though a few basic checks are free.

Also have a look at www.landregisteronline.co.uk which for the grand total of £2 allows you to check who owns what property (again useful in checking out referees).

There are plenty of other sites and more spring up all the time, so do your own searches too.

Managing the property once the tenancy is under way

Doing this yourself is a more realistic proposition. It is common for landlords to employ an agent to find a tenant and then take over the management of the property themselves. But be aware it is far easier to do this if you live within an hour or so of the property. Any further away and you will need a list of reliable plumbers, electricians, roofers, and so on, who are available virtually around the clock. You may also want to find an emergency key holder for the property who lives close by. Some agencies may agree to be a keyholder for a fee.

There could also be times when an agent is able to get a better rent for your property than you can yourself. This may be because they already have a tenant lined up, have links with large employers in your area, or because they have a particularly good name for supplying quality properties.

If you decide to let yourself and not go through an agent, consider joining a landlords' association. These can be useful sources of information and advice. Look at the website of the National Landlords Association www.landlords.org.uk.

Whatever you do, avoid the twin fatal mistakes of letting to a friend or becoming too friendly with your tenant. Remember that there may be times when you will have to be firm. It will be far less embarrassing all round if you keep your relationship with your tenant on a strictly business footing.

THE AGENT'S ROLE IN HELPING SET THE RENT

Regardless of whether you let through an agent, they can still be of help when deciding how much rent to charge. Assuming you are not a charity, you want to set the rent as high as possible to maximise the return on your investment, but at the same time not pitch it higher than the market can bear.

This is never going to be an exact science unless your letting property is identical to others which are already being rented and you can use their rents as a guide.

Otherwise, before contacting agents, look around at the property rental market in your target area and establish what properties of a similar size in a similar road are fetching. Then consider your property:

◆ Does it have any special features which would allow you to charge a higher rent, for example, larger garden, balcony, an extra bathroom, or closer to public transport?

◆ Or does it have anything which may make it slightly cheaper? Does it back on to a railway line, have a dated kitchen or have some tired-looking rooms which need a bit of decorating?

Now contact three or four lettings' agents and ask them to value the property. Which seems reasonable to you?

It is tempting to go with the agent who puts the highest rental value on your house, but be suspicious if it is much higher than any of the other estimates and higher than you were expecting. Also remember that there is little point holding out for a higher rent if your property sits empty for two months while a tenant is found. Will the higher rent compensate you for losing one or even two month's rent? Probably not. Do your own sums, but it is almost certain that you will be better off setting a reasonable rent and filling your property immediately.

The golden rule is not to be greedy.

WHAT HOLIDAY LETTING AGENCIES DO

The decision about whether to use an agency to market your holiday cottage is probably easier to make than on a long-letting property. In the first two or three years you are unlikely to attract bookings for as many weeks as an agency without spending a significant amount of money on advertising, so any money you may save will have to be spent on that.

Also consider that a reputable letting agency will almost certainly be able to consistently ask a higher price for holidays taken in your cottage than you can as an individual. This is because prospective guests are likely to feel happier handing over what could be a lot of money to an established agency, especially if it is one that they have used before, than they are to an unknown individual with an unknown property.

Before the property is holiday let for the first time

Most agencies offer a broadly similar service.

- They can advise on decoration and the style of furniture.
- They will provide an inventory of furniture, kitchenware and other items which you will be expected to supply.
- They will advertise your property and take bookings.
- They will take payment from the guests.

After the holidays begin

- They will pass on to you payment from the guests, usually in two stages, deposit and balance.

- They can advise you on any queries or problems on the day-to-day running of your holiday cottage.

- They can arbitrate between you and the guests if there is a problem.

- They can offer advice on tax issues relating to the letting of your property.

- They offer a regular inspection (usually annually), and will suggest ways of improving or updating the facilities.

Some top end agencies also supply and train housekeepers to look after your property. Expect to pay more for this service.

HOW TO FIND A DECENT AGENT

There is no shortage of holiday letting agencies across the country. Most holiday areas will be covered by several agencies, some small local specialists and other larger regional and national companies.

Big is not necessarily best, but be aware that the larger the agency, the larger its marketing budget is likely to be and the more potential clients they are likely to reach. However, the smaller local agencies can provide a personal touch, will probably have built up a loyal client list going back years and may be able to fill as many weeks as one of the larger agencies. And critically, the booking staff of smaller agencies may well have first-hand knowledge of the properties and can help potential guests make their choice.

When choosing an agency, it is probably best to select one which has on its books similar properties to your own. Do not aim too high. There is no point in trying to sign up with an agency which sells only top-of-the-range holidays in sumptuous, luxuriously appointed properties when your charming but spartan little cottage caters mostly for climbers and walkers on a budget. (In a case like that the agency probably would not take you on anyway.) It makes far more sense to find an agency which sells mostly to the same market you want to go into. That way, you also take advantage of its existing client list.

Bear in mind as well that the more the agency is aiming for the top end of the market, the higher the standards it will expect and the more it will demand from you as the owner.

Almost all agencies have two key ways of selling: their brochure and via the internet. So check the following:

◆ Are both the brochure and website well-written and informative?

◆ Is the brochure glossy, well produced and professional? Are the photographs of a high standard? (The photographs are critical in selling your property.)

◆ Is the website well produced? Is it fast and well-organised?

◆ Is it up to date?

◆ Does it have extra detail that the brochure will not have room for? More photographs? A map showing the exact location of the property? Its availability?

◆ Is the website easy to find on the internet? Check to make sure it appears close to the top of the list when you do a search using a search engine like Google.

Why the agent's website is so important

It is important that the agency you eventually choose has a good website which is updated frequently. There are several reasons for this:

◆ Many people now research and book their holiday entirely online and if your agency does not have a high internet profile you will not reach these potential guests.

◆ An agency website can be updated every minute of the day to reflect the availability of your cottage. And extra seasonal pictures, more detail or changes can be added at the push of a few buttons.

◆ The internet is particularly useful in helping push potential guests towards the increasingly popular out-of-season breaks which you need in order to lengthen your letting season.

◆ It allows people to make late bookings.

You have to reach as many potential guests as possible in order to maximise your number of bookings, and the best way of doing this is via a site which attracts a lot of people or hits. Be suspicious and probably avoid any agency which is not represented in some way on the internet, or is only going through the motions.

The ultimate test is whether an agency's brochure or website is attractive enough to make you want to book your own holiday through it.

AGENCY CHARGES AND CONDITIONS

Unfortunately the higher rents the agencies can demand may sometimes be cancelled out by their commission. The commissions often tend to be higher than the fees charged by an agency specialising in long lets, and anything around 20% of the weekly rate plus VAT is typical. You may sometimes also have to pay an initial one-off registration fee of between £50 and £200. If your property is at the top end of the market, then the commission could be anything up to 50% which would include a full house-keeping service. One-off registration and other contract fees may also be higher.

But because the rents that agencies charge differ greatly depending on their target client and service they offer, a better method of comparison is probably the net weekly rent you would receive multiplied by the likely occupancy rate, rather than a straight comparison between commissions.

Holiday letting agencies may be more reluctant to negotiate discounts on their commissions because they need to be seen to be treating everyone equally.

It is usual to sign up with an agent for a calendar year. Agents prefer you to stay with them for at least two or three years, arguing there is little point in heavily promoting a property if it is only going to be available for a season. Obviously they cannot hold a gun to your head and force you to sign up again if you do not want to, but it does make sense to stick with them for a while in order to give them a proper chance to build up some interest in your property.

Most insist you make your property available for letting right through the peak periods and will restrict your use of it as owner. You may be allowed perhaps a maximum of one or two weeks in the summer and maybe another week during a month in the mid season. In low season, there will probably be fewer restrictions.

If for any reason you want to stop letting mid-season, be aware that some agencies may impose a surcharge to offset the money they have spent preparing your website and brochure entries, and to compensate them for any loss of commission they may have reasonably expected.

SHOULD YOU GO IT ALONE?

After a while, when the first few panicky weeks have passed (the period when you were convinced the guests would hate your cottage and have a terrible holiday), most sane humans sit back, add up how much they have paid their agency in commission and think: 'I can do that myself'. But be patient for a little longer. On the whole it is probably best to let through an agency for at least a couple of years while you learn the business thoroughly.

If you do eventually decide to go it alone you need to think about where to find your guests. People who have previously taken holidays with you are a good start, but before you contact them and offer them the chance to book their holidays directly with you, take a look at the contract you had with your agency. Make sure there is no restrictive clause or any other reference which forbids you from doing this. If there is but you still want to go ahead and try it anyway, speak to a solicitor about whether the clause is legally enforceable and then take a view on whether it is likely the agency would pursue it anyway. Clauses like these never last for ever, so it may just be easier to wait for a decent interval before trying it.

How to market your property yourself will be examined in detail in the next chapter, but for now remember that those former guests will form a vital part of your future selling strategy. These guests have holidayed with you in the past, hopefully enjoyed themselves, and will have told their family, friends and work colleagues about it.

Assuming you let on average 30 weeks a year for three years before deciding to go it alone. That is 90 families or groups, and if each of those 90 families told between them ten people about the fantastic holiday they took at your property, that is a total of almost 1,000 people who are potential guests. Do not forget that it is significantly easier to sell a known, tested and familiar product to people than to cold sell to complete strangers.

Factors to consider when deciding to stick with an agency or do it yourself:

- ◆ Will you be able to let as many weeks as an agency?
- ◆ Will you be able to charge the same prices as an agency?
- ◆ Do you have the time and expertise to let the property yourself?

This last point is especially important:

- You will have to decide on an advertising strategy. When and where are you going to advertise and how much are you going to spend?

- Do you want your own website? Do you know how to build one? If not, are you prepared to pay someone to do it for you?

- At the very least you will probably have to prepare photographs and a mini brochure for your cottage. Do you have the skills to do this yourself? If not, are you prepared to pay someone to do it?

- Are you a good sales person? Each time someone phones, whether to request a brochure or check availability or facilities, you have to sell your property to them, making it sound fabulous and an opportunity not to be missed.

- Are you usually at home to take calls? If you are not there, you may have lost a sale.

- What happens if you want to go away on your own holiday? Who answers the phone then? Remember there is no such thing as an off-season now: people book their holidays 12 months a year.

- How are you going to accept payment for holidays booked? Many people prefer to pay by credit card, but unless you set up an account with a bank to process these payments (which you will be charged for) you will only be able to accept cheques.

- You will have to chase up the writers of cheques which bounce and the people who are late in paying.

◆ What will be your system for taking deposits and then the final balance? What will be the proportion, and when will the payments have to be made?

◆ What about a foolproof system to ensure there are no double bookings or weeks accidentally missed?

◆ Will you accept short breaks if guests only want to stay three or four nights?

◆ What about late bookings?

◆ How are you with paperwork? You will have to send out brochures and initial covering letters, confirmation of bookings' letters and confirmation of payments, reception details and how to find the property, feedback forms for guests to complete once they have taken their holiday, and so on.

◆ Do you have an office or somewhere else at home you can work from? All the stationery, brochures and files will need to be stored somewhere.

◆ Do you have a computer? Are you able to use it competently enough for spreadsheets, Word documents, email attachments, etc?

◆ Many inquiries will come via email. Are you on broadband to stay logged on permanently?

◆ Do you have a fax machine?

◆ How will you cope, without help or agency back-up, if there is a serious complaint from a guest or if there is serious damage to your property?

You may think a lot of the above may not be necessary. Bear in mind, though, you could be expecting your guests to hand over significant sums of money to you. Top end properties sleeping six to eight plus can bring in thousands a week in the summer. For this, guests will want to be assured about the quality of the property they are booking and the professionalism of the service which is being provided.

On the other hand, if you are the owner of that charming but spartan cottage, a glossy brochure or detailed website will not be as necessary. If your six walker or climber guests are paying between them, say, £200 for a week in February, the chances are they will not be as demanding.

Your final decision about whether to stay with an agency or go it alone will almost certainly depend on how you think you can make more money. You may save yourself a couple of thousand pounds a year in agency commissions, but how much more will you have to spend on advertising, stationery and phone bills? Do your sums carefully to make sure your extra costs do not cancel out the commission you are saving.

PRICING YOUR HOLIDAY LETTING PROPERTY
This is more involved than setting a rental value on a long-letting property because there are extra factors to be taken into consideration.

◆ How luxurious is the property?

◆ What is the proportion of bathrooms to bedrooms?

◆ Does it have extra facilities, for example a swimming pool or games room?

- Is the property in a sought-after holiday area?

- Does it have sea views or direct water frontage?

- Will you charge extra if you accept dogs? (It is standard to make a small charge, perhaps £10–£20 per week per dog to cover extra cleaning.)

- What about linen, towels or baby equipment? Some agencies, usually at the budget end of the market, also charge extra for supplying linen and towels (perhaps £3–£5 each per person per week), as well as extra for cots and high chairs (about £10 per item per week).

Then the time of year has to be considered:

- Peak periods (the most expensive) are usually most of July, August and the beginning of September (to coincide with the school holidays), plus Christmas and New Year.

- Mid periods usually include Easter, school half terms and the months of April, May, June, September and October.

- Low periods are essentially what is left, ie November, December (minus Christmas and New Year), January, February and March, unless of course your property is in a winter sports region when many of these months would be highly sought after.

Many agencies offer returning guests a discount, perhaps 5% if they have been back a couple of times to a more generous 10% if they have been returning for longer.

If you have let through an agency in the past then use their prices as a starting point. If you are setting the prices from scratch, then look at every brochure and website of holiday cottages in your region and get a feel for what your competitors are charging.

On the whole, it is probably best to pitch your prices on the low side in the early stages and fill as many weeks as you can. This is because you want to attract as many guests as possible, make sure they have a good holiday and then go home and tell everyone about it. Then, as demand builds, increase your prices until you feel, using your new-found experience, that you have reached the plateau.

5

How to Market Your Property

If you are not going to let your property through an agent or other third party then you will have to market it yourself. This not difficult, but in the short term it may cost you some extra time and money while you learn what works.

LONG LETTING

Standard properties

Unless your long-letting property is large, luxurious and of a high rentable value, or unusual and likely only to appeal to a few prospective tenants, there is little point coming up with a sophisticated marketing strategy. The vast majority of lets should be simple to arrange.

Go first to the property section of the local newspaper which is usually both cheap and effective. It is worth spending a bit extra to ensure your advert is boxed. If you have any say in the lay-out, make sure there is white space around the words. The white space will make your advert stand out. These details should be included in approximately this order, starting from the top:

- location of the property
- brief description (stunning Regency townhouse, city loft), and the number of bedrooms
- whether it is furnished or unfurnished
- any special features, for example, one-minute's walk from tube (or beach), large garden, parking arrangements, quiet
- any restrictions, ie no pets, no smokers
- rent per month
- what the rent includes if anything (perhaps water rates)
- your contact details (usually a telephone number or box number).

Expensive or top end properties
However, if you think your property does deserve something rather more special than an ad in the local paper, then consider putting together a mini-brochure or factsheet.

This does not have to mean a glossy, high-production number that Knight Frank would be proud of; just a side or two of A4 will do consisting of a couple of pictures of your property's best side (maybe the exterior and the living room or kitchen) and some greater detail.

Somewhere near the top of the mini-brochure you may want to elaborate on your property's charms. If you do, keep your creative writing side in check and do not get carried away and start making wild, unsupported claims about your property's history. Be descriptive but also keep it factual.

◆ Describe the number and type of rooms and their rough dimensions (for example, 19-foot master bedroom with en suite bathroom and dressing area, 22-foot drawing room).

◆ Include details of furnishings and fittings (fitted carpets throughout, Aga kitchen designed by X).

◆ Refer to heating arrangements (under floor, gas-fired, open fire in the dining room).

◆ Mention the aspect of the property if it is good (for example south-facing, which is usually best). If it faces due north it may be better to say nothing at all, or perhaps refer to the property as 'cosy' (which it will be because the lights will always be on).

You do not need to be a graphic designer to turn out a decent looking mini-brochure. Anyone moderately competent with a computer can do it, cheaply and quickly. However, if you are not confident about your eye for design, layout or use of colour, then it will probably be worth employing someone to do it for you.

Once you have your mini-brochure, use it to specifically target those people or organisations that you think may be interested in letting your property. This is different to the scattergun approach when you advertise in a local paper or online when everyone, regardless of their suitability or interest, will see it.

Identify local employers with a high turnover of senior staff (hospitals, universities, armed forces' bases, and so on). Make contact with the staff member responsible for employee relocations and send them copies of your mini-brochure. It is also worth sending it out to large industrial and service sector employers in your area, though their staff turnover will probably be lower.

Unusual or niche properties

If your property is that unusual, either in its design or location, then you may need to market it even more specifically and with a little imagination. The mini-brochure or factsheet will still be useful though. For example, if the property is six miles from the nearest road and/or half way up a mountain, then advertise in walking or climbing magazines or websites. Or promote the property as a retreat for meditation or other spiritual purposes.

If it is the property itself which is unusual, then again think about who could take advantage of its qualities. It may be isolated with soaring acoustics which would be perfect for a professional musician, or perhaps it has a serious home gym in the basement which would appeal to an athlete or anyone working in the health and fitness industry.

Remember though, a direct marketing campaign like this is only necessary if you cannot easily let your property conventionally. There is no point going to extra time and trouble if it is typical for its area, of good quality and likely to appeal to a broad section of the market.

HOLIDAY LETTING

Marketing a holiday cottage is hard work because you need to find guests every week or fortnight for as long as you continue doing it. Compare this with a long let when you only need find a single tenant every year or two, or less frequently if you are lucky. Do not be daunted though; marketing your own holiday cottage is achievable and you will save yourself money (at least in the long run), but you need to give some thought about how you are to do it.

It is worth saying right at the beginning of this section that if you are internet-phobic, you will find it difficult to market your holiday cottage on your own and without the help of an agent. It is possible, but you will certainly find it harder and more expensive, and will not be exploiting your holiday cottage's full letting potential.

Probably the only exception to this is if your property fits into some sort of specialist niche market and guests are able to find you by other means. This will be explored later in the chapter.

MARKET RESEARCH

It is tempting to sniff at market research and consider it some sort of gimmick, of use only to soap powder manufacturers or political parties, but do not forget that the more preparation and thought you put into your project initially, then the more likely it is to succeed.

Market research will help you identify:

◆ What sort of guests you are likely to attract.
◆ What they want from their holiday.
◆ How much they are prepared to pay.

Identifying your guests

You need to know who your guests are likely to be so that you can tailor your product or service to them.

The easiest way of doing this is to compile a brief questionnaire and send it to a cross-section of as many people as possible. This should include family members, friends, colleagues, neighbours, friends of friends, and so on, or you could interview these people yourself and use the questionnaire as a prompt. Make it clear you only want brief answers: this will encourage more people to help, and it will also mean you do not have to spend the next month reading long essays. The more people you enlist in your market research, of varying ages and backgrounds, the better.

Questions to include:

- Do you take holidays in self-catering cottages?
- If not, would you consider it?
- If not, why not?

Regardless of whether they do or not:

- Where do you find and book your holidays? (Internet, brochure, word of mouth, etc)
- How much are you prepared to spend?
- What standard of furnishings and fittings would you expect (clean and basic or something rather more luxurious?)
- How far would you be prepared to travel?

Some suggested supplementary questions (depending on people's patience):

- Are en suite bathrooms important to you?
- Hot tubs?
- Open fires?
- Satellite or cable TV?
- DVD player?
- Separate dining room?
- Good children's facilities?
- Personal welcome from the owner?

Finally, include personal questions about those taking part:

- Where do you live?
- How old are you? (Child, young adult, middle-aged, pensioner.)
- What do you do for a living? Or are you retired?
- Your income? (Under £20K, £20–35K, and so on.)
- Are you married?
- With children?
- Grandchildren?
- What are your hobbies or pastimes?
- What newspapers and magazines do you read?
- Do you have pets?
- Do you take them on holiday with you?

At the end of the exercise you should end up with a few key points, for example: everyone likes an open fire; people are prepared to pay between £300 and £700 per week for comfortable accommodation sleeping four; they do not want to travel for more than five hours to reach their destination; elderly people like to take their dog on holiday; parents of young children want high chairs provided, and so on.

Identifying competitors

Market research also means checking up on your competitors. You need to find out who provides what sort of property in your area, how it is furnished, and how much it costs per week. If you do no other market research, then do this. You are wasting your time if you start marketing your holiday cottage with a rental value picked out of thin air. You may benefit from beginner's luck and get it right: but it is more probable you will under-price (which will cost you money) or over-price (which will cost you guests).

And do not forget that your competitors come in all shapes and sizes. They do not necessarily have to be like you, ie private individuals who have a letting cottage in your area. They will also include:

- National Trust properties
- Landmark Trust properties
- letting cottages (and even the stately homes) on large country estates.

Then there are the local indirect competitors who may not let holiday cottages, but who are still chasing the same guests:

- hotels
- guest houses
- holiday parks
- camp sites.

You are also in competition with:

- letting cottages, guest houses, hotels in other parts of the UK
- any other holiday destination anywhere else in the world.

And, unfortunately, you are also technically in competition with anything else the guest may want to spend their money on:

- a new car
- a home extension
- school fees.

Sobering isn't it. Of all the choices on the planet, why would people pick your little property?

Check on the scale of the industry for yourself: do a Google search on 'holiday cottages' and see how many choices it throws up. On the day I tried (January 2006), there were just under five million matches worldwide and about two and a quarter million in the UK alone.

METHODS OF MARKETING YOUR PROPERTY

Because of the intense competition for guests and their money, you have to do everything in your power to make your product (and it is a product) more attractive and enticing than those of your competitors.

Realistically, there is not much you can do if the guest has already decided to revamp the garden or go skiing in Switzerland. But what you can aim for is that, all things being equal, your cottage will be chosen rather than a similar one down the road.

The internet

Access to the internet is essential if you are serious about maximising your property's letting potential. Many people now rely exclusively on the internet to find and book their holidays, so it is dangerous to ignore it. But you would not want to anyway because there are two enormous benefits of advertising online:

◆ You reach far more people than you could ever hope to in any other way. Everyone on the planet who has access to a computer can potentially see your advert.

◆ The internet is remarkably good value. Once you have paid any set-up charges for your website, there are one or two small annual fees and that is it.

You have two choices: join an existing site or build your own.

A professionally-designed website just for you should reasonably cost between £1,000 and £1,500, though a teenager working from their bedroom will do it for probably closer to £500. If you want to make changes to the site yourself (and you probably will, to reflect availability for example), this will cost about a further £500. Once the site has been set up, you need to register its name every two years for a maximum cost of about £40, and arrange the hosting each year (get it put on the internet) for about £200.

If, however, you are baulking at the cost and the hassle, then a far easier option is to go in with a local tourist board, find some other local holiday cottage owners to join up with, or consider buying space on an existing website which is relevant to your property. This could be a site which promotes the local area or one which caters for hobbies or special interests where you could attract like-minded guests, for example walkers or bird watchers.

If you are thinking about teaming up with other local property owners in a co-operative type venture, then you will have to decide whether having a strong joint internet presence will outweigh the disadvantage of sharing a platform with your competitors.

Either way:

- Ensure that when people do an internet search (on something like Google or Yahoo!) your website comes as close as possible to the top of the list. You do not necessarily have to be a large agency or part of an official tourist authority to achieve a top ten listing; but the more appropriate key words in your title, the more hits you have, the more your site is updated and the longer the site has been up, the better chance you will have. You can also pay extra for inclusion at the top, but this can be extremely expensive and almost certainly will not be cost-effective for the individual property owner.

- Make sure there are good links to and from your site. If you are offering a reciprocal or complementary benefit to the other site, then you probably will not have to pay, otherwise expect to be charged.

- Include a good photograph of your property, plus as much detail as you can, on the front or home page. When you are browsing through perhaps hundreds of properties online, what really slows you down (and is therefore irritating) is constantly having to go into a site and dig for basic facts.

Details to include on the front page:

+ Photograph – the best you can manage. If you do not have a digital camera, find someone who does.

+ Location (not an exact address).

+ How many it sleeps (and if space, a breakdown of how: two doubles, one twin, a single plus cot).

+ Brief property description (17th century listed crofter's cottage; contemporary property set in a commanding position on cliffs).

+ Your contact details.

Further details to include on the second page:

+ Description of rooms and their facilities.

+ Price chart.

+ Availability.

+ When short breaks are available (usually out of high season when you arc less likely to be able to book whole weeks). Short breaks are usually charged at the pro-rata week rate.

You do not want to crowd too many facts on the front page: you need to achieve a balance between the page looking good and being informative. If in doubt, err on the side of design and put more facts on page two. Your website designer should be able to advise you.

Whoever builds the site, make sure it is done in such a way that you can amend it easily from home. This is important because you need to constantly update the information on availability. From time to time, the prices will need changing. You may also like to tweak the description of the property or add seasonal photographs.

Newspaper and magazine advertising

The principal advantage of advertising in papers or magazines is that you can more accurately target your potential guests. Your market research will have helped show you what type of people read what type of newspapers, and a lot of it is common sense anyway. There is no point advertising your holiday cottage in *Motorcycle News* if your guests are more likely to be retired, middle-England couples attracted by the local golf clubs or nearby RSPB reserve.

It makes sense to advertise in the travel pages which, in national newspapers, are usually published at weekends. This may not be a cheap option: for example, a four line advert in the Saturday edition of *The Daily Telegraph* costs something approaching £100, though the more adverts you place the cheaper it is. But against the cost, you have to weigh up the advantage of your advert being seen by many thousands of people each week.

Another recognised place to advertise your holiday cottage is *The Lady* magazine. For a typical three or four-line entry, expect to pay between about £30 and £45 per week. Again, there are discounts for series of adverts.

Wherever you advertise, always include your website address if you have one.

It is possible to target even more accurately your potential guests if they are likely to be interested in the same things, for example the arts or gardening. Identify magazines and websites which cater to these interests and check if they will take adverts for holidays. The easiest way to find the magazines or websites is either to do an internet search or simply go into a large newsagent and look at the shelves. The range and number are bewildering, so as long as the interest or hobby is fairly mainstream it should not be too difficult.

Tourist boards
Despite the internet, and the ease that it allows you to do your own research, finding a property via tourist boards is still extremely popular, possibly because of the perception that while they may not be very exciting, their recommendations will at least be safe, tried and tested.

It is usually necessary to join your local tourist board as a member. This will probably cost less than £100 a year, and for this your property gets an entry in a brochure and on a tourist board's official website. Many of these websites get an enormous amount of hits, so this is publicity well worth considering.

Like an agency, there will be minimum standards. Your holiday letting property will be inspected and graded, which you may have to pay extra for, and you will have to ensure it is fitted out to a degree of comfort and that all the usual legal requirements (gas and so on) are met. You will probably take your own bookings.

Word of mouth
The big advantage here is that it is free. Tell absolutely everyone

you can think of that you have a holiday cottage available. Ask them to tell everyone they know.

Because this is not costing you anything you can afford to be generous, so consider offering bribes to anyone who helps you secure a booking.

+ For every serious inquiry you receive, give them £5, a bottle of wine or a big cake.

+ If they get you a cheap week booking, give them up to half a case of wine or £25–£30 cash.

+ If they fill a peak week, this merits a full case or £60–£80 cash.

+ If your property is large and really top of the range, consider increasing the incentive to at least £100 cash. (This is not much when you consider that some properties can fetch thousands of pounds a week in the high season.)

Only do this in the beginning while you are establishing yourself.

Other free publicity

+ Offer a week in your cottage as a competition prize. This will work best in a specialist magazine where you may already be advertising, and where many of the readers could be potential guests.

+ Consider offering a free week to a journalist. Be careful here though: it is unlikely any journalist is ever going to be allowed to write a glowing full page piece purely on the merits of your cottage, no matter how charming. The best you can realistically hope for is a good plug and a picture. Weigh up whether it is worth it.

- Is your holiday cottage exceptionally old or unusual? Anyone famous born there? Anyone famous (dead or alive) ever stayed there? Any babies born unexpectedly there? A garden packed with unique orchids? In short, is there anything there that a journalist could turn into a genuine news item?

- If you have passers-by, put a sign in the window of the cottage saying that it is available for letting.

- Put a notice in the local shop or Post Office.

More ways of selling weeks (especially the cheap ones)
- Offer 5 or 10% discounts to friends and acquaintances (presumably you would not charge family or close friends).

- Sell an off-season week half price to a builder friend (or electrician, carpenter, plumber) in return for a few repairs.

- Offer weeks through an online auction site.

Using local events to promote your property
You should be able to fill your holiday cottage fairly easily during the summer, Easter, school half-terms, Bank Holidays and at Christmas and New Year. The trick is to secure bookings for the rest of the year.

Look around your area and consider what colourful local events take place in the quieter months which you could use to encourage guests to visit then. These could be anything from fairs and carnivals to traditional May Day celebrations, county shows, pre-Christmas markets or harvest festivals. It is even better if they are traditional.

BUDGETING FOR YOUR MARKETING CAMPAIGN

If you plan to advertise in newspapers or magazines, then for the first year budget for about £1,000–£2,000 or 10% of your expected gross income, which ever is the greater. Once you become established and begin to attract repeat bookings, you should be able to spend less.

One of the few disadvantages to the year-round holiday season is that you have to market and advertise year-round as well. Once it was enough to place a few adverts in early spring in order to fill your Easter to end of September letting period, but now you will have to promote your property virtually 12 months of the year.

This means you have to think carefully about when – and indeed if – to place those expensive newspaper adverts. And once again, the internet looks the more attractive option because it is available all the time and effectively free once it has been set up.

WHY YOU PROBABLY NEED A BROCHURE

However you decide to market your property, you will almost certainly need a brochure of one kind or another. Few people will hand over a lot of money on the basis of a fuzzy picture on the internet or a brief three- or four-line advert in a newspaper or magazine. Most will prefer something tangible to look at before making a final decision.

Much of the information on brochures in the long-letting section, applies to holiday cottage lettings, with two exceptions:

◆ It is far more important for this brochure to be professionally designed. Remember that you are not just imparting information: you are selling a holiday, a dream, an image.

◆ The contents of the brochure will stay the same but the emphasis will switch from the practical to the luxury or romance. This means taking out references to the excellent plumbing and referring instead to a hideaway garden just perfect for an alfresco lunch or the four-poster in the master bedroom.

THE IMPORTANCE OF A MAILING LIST

Mailing lists are highly sought after: consider how many times you have been asked to tick a box on a form if you *do not* want your details passed to another related organisation. Companies love lists of people who have already bought a product or service because they may well be interested in buying something similar in the future. This is a far more cost-effective way of promoting a product or service because time is not being wasted trying to cold-sell to people who have absolutely no interest in your product and never will have.

The mailing list you will build up is no exception (but beware of the provisions of the Data Protection Act). Everyone who contacts you for more information on your property, and/or to request a brochure, has one thing in common: they are potentially interested in holidaying in your cottage, *and if they are interested once then they may be interested again.*

Carefully compile your list: every time you receive a serious inquiry or booking, note the inquirer's name, address, email address and any other details you may have. Always ask where they heard about you so you can measure the success of your marketing. Then use the list to send out details of any late availability weeks (especially in the high season), offers on long weekend breaks in spring or autumn, Valentine's Day packages (flowers, champagne and chocolates thrown in) ... Anything you can think up to get those weeks filled.

Also study the list for any patterns in bookings or types of guests which begin to emerge after a time. That too will help with future marketing.

REPEAT BOOKINGS

This is what you have to strive for. Repeat bookings will be your lifeblood. If you do not start attracting them after three or four years then it may be time to consider going back to an agency, because all the money you are saving on commission is being spent on advertising. In some areas (the Isles of Scilly is a good example), guests return to the same property year after year, booking up for the next holiday virtually as soon as the current one is over.

Savings on advertising costs is not the only benefit. Repeat bookers often take more care of your property because of the loyalty they have to it. Cashflow is better and it is also easier to plan for maintenance and improvements if you know well in advance what your bookings and income will be for the coming year.

How to attract the repeat bookers

♦ Offer them a discount on their holiday. Five or 10% is usual.

♦ Offer them welcome back gifts, an extra special bouquet of flowers, good bottle of wine, etc.

♦ Send personalised (not pre-printed) Christmas cards to remind them you still exist.

- If the guests have returned three or four times consider birthday cards, especially for children, but do not overdo it.

- Maintain an emailing list, keeping guests up to date with improvements to your property (good news – a third bathroom!) plus any other local news which may be relevant to them (local adventure park re-opens).

IS IT ALL WORTH IT?

After considering this chapter and your own position, sit down and think about whether it really is worth going to all the time and trouble of marketing your own property or if it is best left in the hands of an agency.

The arguments can be distilled to these:

- If you are short of time and you do not have to count every penny, then leave it to an agency.

- If you have spare time, are prepared to do the paperwork and are considering adding more properties to your holiday letting portfolio in future, then do the marketing yourself.

6

The Long-Letting Landlord

T he big decision in this chapter is whether to let your property furnished or unfurnished.

FURNISHED VERSUS UNFURNISHED

There is an increasing demand for unfurnished properties, perhaps because many people will have acquired at least some furniture, ornaments and pictures by the time they are in their late twenties. There are also the divorcees who will have kept some family furniture, and others who are between houses and will want to keep their possessions with them. And there are those who are choosing not to buy, for whatever reason, and are staying instead in the private rented sector, especially because it is far more buoyant and 'respectable' than it was a decade or two ago.

If possible, it is probably best to let your property unfurnished. It is significantly cheaper and far less bother because there is no initial financial outlay, nothing to replace or repair when items wear out or break, and no white goods to service or otherwise be responsible for.

Also, as a general rule, letting unfurnished will probably not make much difference to the rent you can charge, though do check with letting agents near you because there will be local factors to consider. You need to make a minimum of about an extra £70–£75 a week for it to be worthwhile.

One of these factors may be the existence of a thriving corporate let market, usually letting to companies on behalf of their transient employees. These markets are almost always in the larger cities, particularly London.

There could be other reasons why you would prefer to let your property furnished. Maybe you already have an existing collection of good furniture, curtains, crockery and kitchen items which would otherwise be costing you money to keep in storage. The key word here is 'good'. Do not let your property furnished simply because you have a load of junky old furniture which you cannot bring yourself to throw away. Poor quality furniture will, on the whole, attract poor quality tenants and there will be less incentive for them to look after your property.

If you let furnished, consider hanging pictures on the walls. This will discourage people from putting up their own pictures, making more holes and damaging the plaster. But again, make sure they are decent pictures in keeping with the style of the property.

Letting your property part-furnished is the other option. It is perfectly acceptable to provide carpets and curtains, kitchen white goods, and perhaps beds and a sofa, but you have to ask yourself if there is much point when you may be able to ask the same rent by not providing anything at all. Some landlords may consider part-furnishing to be the worst of both options.

In all cases, local market forces will determine demand, so seek advice near you.

MINIMUM TO PROVIDE IF YOU FURNISH

If you decide to let your property furnished, you need to start thinking about what to provide and how much it is going to cost you quite early on and certainly long before you complete on the house or flat purchase. This is because:

- it will take far longer than you think to buy everything you need
- the order time for larger items like sofas and beds can be up to ten or twelve weeks.

What you need to aim for is to have all the furniture and fittings assembled and ready to be moved into your property the moment the decorating and cleaning have been finished. Your investment property should be empty and therefore earning no money for the shortest possible time, and the only way to achieve this is to think ahead.

The following is a suggested list of basic items to provide. There is a more comprehensive list in the next chapter on furnishing a holiday cottage.

Assume it is a two/three-bedroomed property:

Item	Approximate cost
Carpets, lino and/or floor tiles throughout, including fitting and laying	£1,000–£2,500
Curtains, poles and blinds throughout	£400–£1,000
Lampshades, or equivalent, throughout	£100–£300
Smoke alarms	£25–30
Carbon monoxide detector	£20
Fire extinguishers and fire blanket	£150–£200

Reception room

Sofa and easy chairs	£1,000–£,1500
TV and DVD/video (optional)	£250–£500
Coffee/side tables	£150–£400
Side lamps	£100 £250
Miscellany (cushions, pictures, ornaments)	£250–£750
Table and chairs (for four)	£250–£750

Per bedroom

Double bed and mattress	£300–£600
Bedside cabinets (× 2)	£50–£200
Wardrobe	£150–£250
Chest of drawers	£75–£250
Bedside lights (× 2)	£30–£100
Mirror	£10–£40

(It is not usual to supply duvets, pillows or bed linen.)

Kitchen

Cooker	£300–£600
Fridge/freezer	£180–£400

Item	Approximate cost
Microwave	£50–£150
Dishwasher	£200–£450
Washing machine	£200–£400
Tumble dryer	£150–£300
Toaster and kettle	£35–£75
Pots, pans, roasting trays, grill pan	£100–£250
Mixing bowls	£20–£50
Lasagne, pie and vegetable dishes	£50–£100
Crockery (dinner and side plates, bowls)	£75–£300
Cups and saucers and mugs	£50–£150
Cutlery	£20–£100
Glasses	£15–£75
Cooking utensils: knives, wooden spoons, corkscrew, tin opener, cheese grater, etc	£50–£150
Vacuum cleaner	£40–£300
Iron and ironing board	£30–£75
Washing up bowl, bucket, dustpan and brush, inside bins and dustbins	£100–£200
Total	£5,975–£13,765

You can do it more cheaply if you buy the crockery and kitchenware at markets, go for bottom-of-the-range white goods and buy all your large furniture in the cheapest discount stores. But it will probably be a false economy because the goods will not last as long.

If you are going to go for fully furnished, you will have to start buying everything while the property purchase is going through and therefore exactly at the time when you will already be paying out for legal fees, stamp duty and so on. So how is your cash flow? Will you have a further £6,000-plus to spare for the furnishings? And do you have the time to source and buy everything yourself? If not, you will probably have to pay someone to do it for you.

It does not matter how carefully you budget for furnishings: it always costs more than you think, so mentally add on another 10% for contingencies.

GETTING AHEAD OF YOURSELF

Every day that your property stands empty costs you money, so try to negotiate as long a period as possible between exchange and completion on the deal to give yourself more time to get everything in place.

If the property is already empty, check to see if the vendors will allow you access to clean and decorate between exchange and completion. There should be virtually no risk in doing this: your solicitor should confirm that once contracts have been exchanged, nothing short of a direct hit from a meteor would stop the deal going through.

Also check to see if the vendors are prepared to allow you to show prospective tenants around during this limbo period between exchange and completion. If so, then you can have your furniture ordered, property redecorated and a tenant lined up and ready to move in the moment completion has happened.

TENANCY AGREEMENTS

A good contract is the key to a successful landlord/tenant relationship.

There is one tenancy system for Scotland and one for England, Wales and Northern Ireland. The differences are not enormous and some of the main points are covered here, but talk to a letting agent or solicitor if you are not sure.

In Scotland, landlords and tenants enter into a Short Assured Tenancy. These agreements are issued initially on a six-month lease. Towards the end of the term, the agent or owner will write to the tenant to ask whether they want the Agreement to continue. If they do, then an extension is issued, usually for another fixed period (though it does not have to be for six months). If the landlord wants possession, he or she must give the tenant at least two months' notice to leave, and the due date must coincide with the end of the lease. If the tenant wants to go, they only have to give a month's notice. If nothing happens when the six-month lease expires, then the agreement defaults to something called 'tacit relocation' and things continue pretty much as they were anyway.

The remainder of this section refers to the situation in England, Wales and Northern Ireland. The name of the agreement is different, but otherwise there are similarities in the two systems.

In England, Wales and Northern Ireland, the landlord and tenant will enter into an Assured Shorthold Tenancy Agreement (known as an AST). If, however, your property has a rental value of more than £25,000 a year (not unusual in central London) you cannot use an AST: instead you sign a straight contract which means a different section of the law will apply. In practice it should not make that much difference, but you should speak to a letting agent or solicitor with experience in this field.

Make sure your Agreement is for a period of not less than six months. There is no maximum length, but it is probably safer to make sure it does not last any longer than 12 months at a time. If you do agree a term of less than six months, note that the law does not allow the landlord to end the contract until six months after the start date anyway.

After the initial term of the Agreement it is not necessary to formally renew it. Instead it lapses to something called a 'periodic tenancy', and in practice everything continues in exactly the same way.

(It is not ideal for a six month Agreement to expire just before Christmas because you will probably have to wait until the holiday period is over before finding replacement tenants. That means your void or non-income earning period will be longer than necessary. Instead, consider making the Agreement seven months initially so it lapses after the holiday period, perhaps around the first or second week in January.)

You can reissue the contract every six months (or whatever the fixed term is) if you want to, but there is little point doing this unless you want to change the terms of the Agreement or you want to try to commit your tenant to staying for a further fixed period.

What the Agreement should do is set out exactly what is expected from both sides, removing any opportunities for misunderstandings. However, if your tenant fails to comply with any aspect of the Tenancy Agreement and you want to regain possession of your property, then the Agreement provides the legal framework to help you do so.

Under some circumstances the Agreement should be stamped by
HM Revenue & Customs (the old Inland Revenue) which
effectively validates it. The rules changed in December 2003 and
it is no longer necessary to do this unless your tenants are like to
stay for a long time and/or the annual rentable value of the
property is likely to be high. Most landlords will not be affected:
if in doubt, check.

There are essentially three ways of having the contract drawn up:

- Employing a letting agent who will do it for you.
- Employing a solicitor who will do it for you.
- Buying an off-the-shelf pack from a stationer.

Using an agent or solicitor will obviously be more expensive, but
the Agreement will be drawn up to reflect your own
circumstances and the detail it includes may be more useful if, for
any reason, you ever have to go to court. The packs cost around
£10 each.

WHAT TO INCLUDE IN A TENANCY AGREEMENT

The Agreement should state the address of the property, your
name and address and that of the tenants. It should include the
start date of the tenancy, the rent and which day it is due, and
the amount of deposit required. (One or two months' rent is
standard: if there is a lot to damage, go for as much as you can.)
If the property is furnished, the Agreement can also refer to the
inventory of contents which should be attached as an appendix.

Tenant's obligations

The Agreement should compel the tenant to look after the
property and its contents. The tenant should also not be allowed

to make any alterations to the property without the landlord's consent; be a 'nuisance' or 'annoyance'; do nothing illegal; and do nothing which may affect the validity of any insurance policies held.

Method of payment
Always insist on a bank standing order for rent. It is usual for it to be paid a month in advance. Make sure the contract states this.

Rent arrears and breakages
Ensure the contract makes it clear you intend to recoup any reasonable sums from the deposit to cover costs incurred in trying to recover rent arrears, unpaid utility bills or breakages.

The Tenancy Agreement should also state that the tenant is in breach if the rent is more than 14 days late. However, failure to pay the rent does not automatically allow the landlord to regain possession of the property: it is still necessary to go to court to obtain an order.

Inventory
The contract should state that the tenant should check the inventory and return a signed copy within a fixed period, say a week, of moving in. Anything missing from the inventory at the end of the Tenancy Agreement will be deducted from the deposit.

Keys
Also make sure the contract states you will deduct a sum from the deposit if the tenant fails to return keys and the locks need to be changed. Depending on the area of the country and level of security necessary, this could be expensive (up to a few hundred pounds) so it is important not to overlook this.

Repairs

The contract should make it clear that the tenant cannot arrange repairs without prior permission from you or your agent.

It should also make it clear that the tenant is liable for any cost incurred in calling out a plumber, electrician or similar, because of a breakage or other fault caused originally by the tenant.

Maintenance

The contract should compel the tenant to maintain the property in a good condition throughout the life of the tenancy. They should hand the property back at the end of the tenancy in the same condition as it was at the start. The reasonable cost of any remedial works necessary to bring it back up to standard will be deducted from the deposit.

Garden

It should be made clear who is responsible for maintaining the garden and other outside areas. If it is the tenant's responsibility and they neglect that, then the cost of any remedial work to return the outside areas to their original state will be deducted from the deposit.

Decorating

It is safest to ban the tenant from carrying out any decorating without your prior written permission. If you want to be more lenient then you could allow the tenant to decorate in their own taste on the condition that they return the property to its original condition before they leave. If they do not, then the cost of any remedial work will be deducted from the deposit.

Returning the deposit

The contract should state the terms for returning the tenant's deposit. It is usual for it to be returned within a month, which will allow all the above checks to be made and for any money owing to be deducted.

Make sure the contract clearly states that the deposit cannot be used to cover the tenant's final rent payment.

Bills

It should be made clear which bills the tenant is responsible for. The landlord must pay the buildings insurance, if only to make sure it is done, and contents cover too if the property is let furnished. The tenant is usually responsible for the remainder of the bills, including council tax, electricity, gas, oil, phone, water, any other utilities and TV licence. Make sure you or your agent take meter readings when tenants move in and out.

Either you or your agent should notify the utility companies of your tenant's name and the date that they became responsible for the bills. This is the safest way to make sure it is done, so do not leave it to the tenants.

Sub-letting

It is probably best to forbid this outright unless you give the tenant separate formal written permission. It is difficult to think of a circumstance where sub-letting without prior permission could be anything but disastrous for the landlord.

Access

If you are feeling particularly cautious you may also want to include a clause on the landlord's right of access to the property. This is largely a matter of common sense: if it is routine maintenance then a written seven-day notice period should be sufficient (48 hours' notice is the minimum); if it is a dire emergency and the tenant is absent, then it will probably be immediate.

Under access also include a condition that the outgoing tenants must allow you to show prospective replacement tenants around the property.

Other restrictions

Depending on the nature of your letting property, you may also want to use the contract to restrict the tenant in other ways. This may include the maximum number of people allowed to live there, the type and number of pets they can keep, and the type and number of vehicles allowed to be parked on the property and their condition (for example, no commercial vehicles, only two domestic-use cars which must be roadworthy).

You may want to state that the property should only be used as a home and that no businesses or trade should be operated from there.

Also consider a clause that the tenants should not leave the house unoccupied for a fixed period (for example more than a fortnight) without informing you or your agent in writing. This is particularly relevant in inner cities or remote areas where burglary may be a problem, or in colder or more exposed regions where frozen pipes or other interrupted supplies are possible in winter. So the contract should say that the tenant has to ensure that the property is protected from frost, fire, water damage or entry by unauthorised people.

If the property has particularly well fitting doors or windows, also consider a clause which compels the tenant to provide adequate ventilation. Opening windows, especially in steamy areas, may seem basic but a surprising number of people do not do it, and mould quickly builds up on the inside of window frames, on walls and sometimes on bathroom carpets (not a good idea anyway).

The above is only a guide on what to include and is not an exhaustive list. If you are not sure about what to include yourself, then employ an agent to do it for you.

If you are new to letting then the list may sound draconian. In practice most tenants are reasonable and will expect to sign a formal contract because it gives them a degree of protection as well. Few tenants turn out to be monsters and it will rarely be necessary to enforce anything, especially if you have carefully selected your tenant in the first place, taken up references and made it perfectly clear what is expected from both sides.

Ultimately you cannot be too precious about your property. There is no such thing as the perfect tenant, and a degree of wear and tear is almost inevitable. It is up to you to learn to live with it, and an agent will certainly help by being a buffer between you and the other side. But if, after having tried letting, you cannot happily accept the constant small niggles, breakages and general deterioration, you need to ask yourself if you are in the right game.

The landlord's obligations

It is sensible to include in the contract your own obligations as landlord. These are very much in your interests anyway.

Essentially you must agree to keep in good repair the property and contents, including the supply of water, gas, electricity and sanitation facilities.

You must also agree to insure the property and any contents listed on the inventory, and use all reasonable efforts to replace them as soon as possible in the event of an insured incident.

You also have to agree that your tenant may live in your property without unnecessary interruption or harassment.

Notice period

The agreement should also state the notice period. The landlord is legally required to give at least two months' notice and the tenant has to give at least one. It should be made clear in the Tenancy Agreement how much notice the landlord requires and how it should be given, ie in writing to the address on the notice letter. Usually the tenant cannot give notice before the end of the initial fixed period (typically six months). But this is when it can start getting complicated, and ideally an agent or solicitor should be consulted.

Inspections

Quarterly visits are standard. These inspections should not be a problem as long as the tenant is told about them when they take on the Agreement and that they are conducted diplomatically. The regular inspections should benefit all parties:

◆ As landlord you can check how well the property has been looked after.
◆ You can discuss with the tenant any worries you may have.
◆ The tenant can discuss with you any worries they may have.

- ◆ You can discuss what remedial work is necessary.
- ◆ You can discuss if any item of furniture needs replacing.

Rent rises

You will probably want to include a clause in the contract which says when the rent is due for review: this is usually on or about the anniversary of the start of the Tenancy Agreement. Do not commit yourself to a firm date or formula to decide the rise. Economic and other circumstances change so keep your options open.

When you have decided on a rent rise, write to the tenant and tell them your decision. Look at what rents are doing in your area and set the increase accordingly. If you really are stuck on what would be a fair increase, just add on the inflation rate or annual £25 or £50 increments. Remember that it is far better to err on the low side in order to keep a good tenant, rather than going through the hassle of finding another one and running the risk of voids, all for another few pounds a month.

These suggested points to include in a Tenancy Agreement are not definitive because each owner's circumstances will be different. So you must seek professional advice if you are in any doubt about your own position.

CLEANING AND DECORATING

Common sense will tell you that the better condition the property is in when it is handed over to a tenant, the more likely they are to look after it. If it is scruffy, poorly painted, with chipped woodwork and dirty kitchens and bathrooms, then there is far less incentive for them to do so. Also, a decently decorated property is likely to attract a better tenant.

Between tenants

◆ Paint the walls (or at the very least touch up scuffed or marked paintwork). Pay particular attention to the areas around light switches, just above stair treads and in the kitchen, especially near the bin and above the cooker where there may be fat or other food stains. Re-painting is not a major capital investment so this is worth doing properly. Neutral pastels are safest.

◆ Check all windows open smoothly and then clean them.

◆ Bleed the radiators and make sure there are no air locks.

◆ Thoroughly clean the kitchen and bathroom, including the bits you normally avoid. In the bathroom this means scouring behind the loo pan and sink pedestal, the skirting boards behind the door, and the tiles above the shower head. In the kitchen, pay particular attention to tiles, the cracks where work surfaces join or meet the walls, and the seals on the fridge and freezer doors. If the task is so huge or depressing then employ a cleaning company to blitz the place.

◆ Consider replacing carpets if they are badly stained. If they are lightly marked then it may be possible to spot treat them yourself, or you could have them cleaned professionally. That will bring better results initially, but be aware that carpets which have been too thoroughly wetted and cleaned can sometimes be more vulnerable to marking in the future.

◆ Consider washing or dry cleaning the curtains, though unless your tenants were particularly dirty or had been there a long time this may not be necessary.

◆ Check the TV aerial is working, correctly aligned and picking up channels.

- If furnished, check furniture, especially mattresses and other upholstered items. Spot clean if necessary or consider replacing them.

- Check all crockery, glasses and pans for chips, cracks and marks. Replace as necessary.

During a tenancy

Clearly it is in no one's interests to clean or decorate annually during the life of a tenancy. The tenant will probably not want the disruption and you will not want the expense. If cleaning or decorating is really that necessary, then perhaps it is time to consider changing your tenants.

If your tenant is well behaved, then thorough decorating is probably only necessary every four or five years, especially if it was done properly in the first place. It should be possible to do it between tenancies.

ROUTINE MAINTENANCE

You will probably have to carry out routine maintenance far more frequently than you do with your own home. As a landlord you have legal obligations to protect your tenants and their visitors. These requirements are explained in detail in Chapter 11, but what it boils down to is that you have a responsibility to ensure that all appliances powered by gas, oil or electricity are safe, and to ensure this they have to be inspected and tested at regular intervals by qualified engineers.

CORPORATE LETTING

This is a more specialised area and if you are considering it then find an agent who has experience in this field. But points to bear in mind for now are:

- ◆ Only consider corporate letting if your property is in London, areas of the Home Counties with good commuter links, or in other cities where there are large employers with mobile staff and probably overseas offices.

- ◆ Assured Shorthold Tenancy Agreements can only be signed by individuals and not companies. If the contract is to be between you and an employee then it is all right to use one. If however the agreement is to be between you and the employer then a contract will be needed. Companies which use corporate lets sometimes have their own draft contracts which, of course, may be drawn up in their favour so take advice.

- ◆ Occasionally companies may want to pay the rent in advance for up to two or three years. In return you are expected to reduce the rent slightly.

- ◆ Fittings and furnishings will usually have to be of a high standard.

It is probably safer letting to companies, especially if they are well known and with reputations to protect, but you may have to work harder for your money.

DISABLED ACCESS

In October 2004 a new part of the Disability Discrimination Act 1995 came into force. It mainly impacts on commercial premises where landlords or service providers will be under an additional duty not to treat the disabled less favourably. If you think you may be affected then talk to a local letting agent with experience in this field.

WHY IT IS IMPORTANT TO KEEP GOOD TENANTS

If your tenants keep your property clean and tidy and pay their rent on time, do everything reasonable to keep them for as long as possible. Long standing tenants mean:

- fewer 'void' weeks (the period between tenants when your property is standing empty and therefore earning no money)

- fewer occasions when you have to find tenants (agencies can charge several hundred pounds for a 'tenant find')

- fewer 'in and outs' which means less removals' damage and less disruption.

New tenants are an unknown quantity which is enough to make any landlord nervous. It also means:

- a potential for more breakages because they will be unfamiliar with the central heating, hot water and other appliances

- potential damage to walls and decoration because they will hang pictures in different places and shift furniture around.

Unfortunately there is no way of knowing how long a tenant will stay. Even if they do agree to stay for a fixed period, circumstances still change. Families break up, people change jobs or are relocated by their employers. So consider as a bonus each month over the initial six months that a good tenant is still there.

HOW TO KEEP YOUR TENANTS HAPPY

An average tenancy lasts 16 months according to ARLA (the Association of Residential Letting Agents).

Above all, tenants want things to *work*. Common sense should tell you that if something does not work properly, the tenants will become frustrated and less likely to look after the property well, while you as landlord will only be postponing the inevitable because you will have to get it fixed eventually anyway.

The two key areas here are maintaining high standards of fittings and furnishings (if furnished) and providing a professional management service. So:

◆ provide a decent kitchen and bathroom
◆ have your property decorated to a professional standard
◆ if something breaks, fix it promptly but appropriately (a malfunctioning boiler should be sorted out immediately: a dripping outside tap can wait a few days)
◆ be courteous to your tenants or ensure your agent is
◆ at all costs avoid arguments.

If you are furnishing your property:

◆ provide decent, good quality furnishings
◆ if your tenant asks for something reasonable (a new washing machine to replace a clapped out one) then try to provide it.

But while it is important to do everything reasonable to keep a good tenant, it is equally important not to be too accommodating. Some novice landlords fall into the easy trap of being too generous and desperate to please. So keep reminding yourself that your tenants are not your personal house guests, you are in charge and that you are letting your investment property for your benefit and not theirs.

It is all a matter of striking the right balance.

Privacy

Most tenants want to be left alone: they do not want to be bothered or feel hassled by you. If you do not hear from them, conclude that everything is OK. Call or contact them only when strictly necessary. Do not drop by unexpectedly. Never let yourself in using your own key unless it is a real emergency.

7

Furnishing a Holiday Cottage

C leaning up after the previous owners, doing whatever building
work is necessary, redecorating and furnishing will take far
longer than you think, so under no circumstances accept your first
bookings unless you are absolutely sure you will be ready,
especially if you are relying on builders or other outside help. Even
when you think you have a date to finish, add on a fortnight for
snags: this is the time to re-hang curtains because they do not fall
properly, add cabin hooks to irritating doors which will not stay
open and clear out all your DIY tools.

The last couple of days before your first guests arrive will be
terrifying because it is like the run-up to the largest party you
have ever given, multiplied by 100. Much of the responsibility for

your guests having a great holiday lies with you, but if you do not give yourself enough time to prepare, the anxiety levels will be even worse.

HOW TO DECORATE

Furnishing and equipping the inside is as important as buying the right property in the first place. If it does not look or feel right, the guests will not be comfortable and you will not get those vital repeat bookings. Furnishings and decoration are obviously a matter of individual taste, but there are still some important rules.

◆ Firstly, and most importantly, it must have character. Blandness, everything beige, is the worst look to end up with.

◆ White or off-white emulsioned walls and ceilings are best, especially if the property is old. (Gardenia is apparently the new magnolia.) Walls, even in the most expensive and well-looked after properties, mark quickly. This is a particular problem around the front door, the staircase where people carry suitcases up and down, and in the kitchen around the bins. Emulsion can be touched up easily and dries within an hour on a reasonable day. Repairing rips or removing marks on wallpaper is far more difficult.

◆ White walls and ceilings will allow you to have strong colours for carpets, rugs, sofas and curtains. You need strong colours to hide minor marks and stains. Patterns are all right if they are discreet, but remember that on the whole any sort of design or pattern tends to date more quickly.

◆ Hang decent pictures, the most expensive you can afford. They should be safe enough on the walls, away from accidental breakages.

- Ornaments and photographs. This is difficult to get right. Do not use your investment property as a dumping ground for your own unwanted trinkets. A few decent ornaments and even photographs of your family can be homely, but remember that you or your housekeeper have to dust around them, and at all costs do not overdo it because nothing looks worse than someone else's clutter.

- Cottage style. It is easy, especially with an older property, to go for the flowery, chintzy look. Be careful if you take this path. In moderation there is nothing wrong with it, but it may deter men (it is not always the woman who chooses the holiday) and can look very 1980s.

- Local colour. When choosing furnishings, try to reflect the surroundings. This does not mean all pictures have to be seascapes or furniture made out of driftwood if you are by the sea. Instead, invest in a few good examples of local work and then add some other more neutral pieces.

- Finally, think hard about the character, style and age of your house before furnishing it. You do not have to only put contemporary furniture in modern homes, or antiques in older properties. Mixing and matching is fine, but try to maintain a couple of common themes, which could be colour or the use of a similar wood or metal.

HOW MUCH TO SPEND

This will depend on two factors: the type of guest you would like to attract and the depth of your pocket.

- Option one is to do it as cheaply as possible while still buying new. This means beds and other furniture from discount stores, and crockery and glasses, pots and pans from markets. If you take the cheap option, it will show. Do not expect to attract guests prepared to pay a top rate. You will also have to replace items more often. Do not, under any circumstances, buy furniture second hand unless you are sure it meets current fire safety regulations.

◆ Option two is the middle way. Take this route and you will spend a lot of time in stores like John Lewis and Habitat. Just remember that many of your guests will have been in exactly the same shops, will know the prices and may well have the same things at home, only in a better condition.

◆ Option three means hand-made kitchens, bone china and French bed linen. Do this by all means if you can afford it, but make sure you have a property to match and will be able to charge high enough rents to justify it.

Common sense tells you that option two is probably the best, with bits of one and three thrown in. Crudely, the more you invest in decent, good quality furniture and fittings, the more you can charge. Remember that self-catering holidays in the UK are not cheap. A fortnight in a cottage in August for a family of four can cost significantly more than a thousand pounds, and that is just the accommodation. Guests prepared to pay that will often be high earners who live in expensive properties themselves, and will have high expectations to match.

Do not forget to haggle over prices, or look for discounts if you spend over a certain amount.

WHAT TO BUY

Brace yourself because this is going to be a long and expensive list. But remember that your expenses are tax deductible which means you will pay less income tax on your eventual profits. This is explained in more detail in Chapter 14, but for now the only thing you have to remember is to keep all your receipts.

The approximate range of costs are in bold at the end of each mini-section. Assume a holiday cottage sleeping four.

The big purchases

Flooring
You have to decide this right at the beginning because what you have will dictate almost everything else.

Carpets – pros and cons
✓ they are warm
✓ they absorb noise
✓ they are kinder to small, crawling children
✗ they need replacing more frequently
✗   they can harbour dust mites
✗ they are not popular with asthma sufferers.

Bare boards – pros and cons
✓ it does not matter so much if drinks/food are spilt
✓ it does not matter so much if guests walk mud through the
    house
✓ boards are harder wearing
✗ they are noisy
✗ you will have to buy rugs
✗ fluff and dust gather quickly in obvious clumps
✗ they need sanding and re-sealing every five to seven years.

The decision may be made for you by the style of the house or what you have been left by the previous owners. If you go for carpets, pick a warm and deep colour (but not 1970s swirly). Or there are excellent value, oatmeal/specked beige wool carpets on the market. Even if nothing catastrophic is spilled on them, they will still need replacing every three to five years.   **£1,000–£2,500**

Sofa(s) and armchairs

There needs to be enough for all your guests to sit down in comfort at the same time. You do not have to buy a three-piece suite but try to maintain a theme, for example the same shades or style. The sofa and chairs have to be good quality to withstand some hard wear and tear.

Do not go for feather-stuffed cushions because they need properly shaking up every night if they are not to become compacted and hard (and you cannot rely on or expect guests to do that). Instead, go for best quality foam or latex stuffings which maintain their shape and are more comfortable anyway. Make sure the fabric is hard-wearing. Leather can look chic and is easy to clean, but it is cold and not something you fancy snuggling into on a wet stormy night.

Whatever you go for, it is going to be one of your biggest purchases, but looked after properly should last at least five to seven years.   **£750–£2,000**

Tables and chairs

Some houses will be large enough to have a table in the kitchen and a separate dining room. In at least one of these rooms there should be a large table and enough chairs for everyone to sit down and eat together. The table tops should be wipeable.

Even if you provide tablecloths do not assume they will be used. On tables used by children, be prepared for felt tip pen marks and dents where they bang cutlery. There may well be cigarette burns from adults enjoying long, boozy dinners. A table with a battered top can in the right property add character: there is, however, a thin but distinct line between character and scruffy.

£250–£750

Beds

This you have to get absolutely right. Beds are personal so they have to be spotless. Buy the best you can afford.

Slatted bases are probably better than divans. Guests can keep suitcases under slatted beds and the air can circulate underneath. You can also vacuum under them and it is easier to dust the wooden or metal frames.

Do not buy soft or hard mattresses: you cannot please everyone all of the time so you might as well try to please the majority most of the time by providing ones of medium comfort. If a mattress gets stained, throw it out. It does not matter if it is the most innocent stain in the world, or if it is hidden under a mattress protector, because some guests will check. Assuming the mattress is of a decent quality and the bed is slept in 30–40 weeks a year, consider replacing the mattress every four to eight years.

£300–£600 each

Bed linen

Cheap bed linen quickly bobbles, so buy the best you can afford. It is difficult to go wrong with 100% cotton.

As far as the colour is concerned, there are two schools of thought. All-white linen never fades, can be boiled up and everything always matches, but it shows every peg mark and speck of dust. Coloured bed linen adds more colour and warmth to a room but usually begins to fade after multiple washes. Whatever you decide, try to aim for a cosy and warm feel in the bedrooms without being too Parisienne boudoir.

Bed linen comes under the heading of Big Purchases because you are going to need a lot of it:

- one duvet per bed
- four pillows per double/king size bed, and two pillows per single, plus a couple of extras. Provide one feather and one foam-filled pillow per sleeper to cover all preferences and allergy conditions
- one washable mattress protector per bed plus one spare
- waterproof mattress protector if you are accepting young children
- one pillow protector for each pillow plus two spare. Zipped ones are best because they do not wrinkle under pillow cases
- minimum of three duvet covers, each with matching pillow cases, per bed*
- minimum of three white sheets per bed*
- minimum of six white pillow cases per double bed, or three per single.*

£750 approx

*You need all this duplicate bed linen to cover the periods when guests stay for a fortnight. Often, linen for both weeks is left with them: therefore you will need the third set for the week after the fortnighters have left. If you have two fortnight bookings back to back, you may need a fourth set.

You can go down the sheets, blankets and bedspread route but most guests will not expect it. You or your housekeeper will have to regularly air the blankets so it is probably easier to stick with duvets.

The big purchases – luxury optionals

One man's luxury is another man's essential. There is no definitive list of what *has* to be provided. You will have to take your own view, depending on the type of market you are going into. But once again remind yourself that the more and better you provide, the more you can charge. And also remember that if all things are equal between yours and a similar property down the road, one little extra luxury could tip a booking in your favour.

◆ Satellite TV. You may be unsure personally, but there are millions of people (men) out there who would sooner leave their children behind than go on holiday without being able to watch televised football, especially during the big tournaments. It is also useful in an area where TV reception may be poor.

◆ Digibox/Set Top Box.

◆ DVD player. Another almost-essential, particularly since they are now so cheap.

◆ Four poster bed. Still very popular, and despite what you think, not just with guests under 40.

- Sauna/jacuzzi/hot tub/double shower. Not exactly furniture, but something to consider when thinking about added luxuries. Many people take holidays simply to relax and do absolutely nothing. In the right property, these are a big draw.

Essential white goods and electrical items

- Fridge and freezer (or combined). These have to be large enough to realistically cope with the number of guests you accept. Families in particular use freezers a lot. **£180–£400**

- Cooker and hob (if not built in). **£300–£600**

- Washing machine. A modern one with a high spin speed and half-wash option will save you money in the long run. Families, especially with small children, will do lots of washing. **£200–£400**

- Tumble dryer. Separate tumble dryers are often more efficient than washer-dryers (unless you go for something top-of-the range). A washing machine with a high spin speed means the washing which goes into the tumble dryer should not take as long to dry. **£150–£300**

- Dishwasher. Essential because many people would not dream of renting a holiday cottage without one. It is also useful on changeover days if anything needs another going over, and you or your housekeeper do not have time to do a sinkful of dishes. **£200–£400**

- Microwave. Another must have. **£50–£150**

- Toaster and kettle. These are two of the most visible and most used items in the kitchen and therefore not the place to scrimp on money. **£35–£75**

With all white goods buy the best you can afford. Rusty and noisy appliances do not inspire confidence in guests paying top-of-the range prices.

Other kitchen essentials

Buying good quality, well-designed kitchen and tableware does matter. Many guests have low expectations of what they expect to find in self-catering cottages, so surprise them and it will pay off. They will appreciate it, comment on it, on the whole look after it (anyone can smash a wine glass) and will remember it when it comes to booking the following year's holiday.

If possible, try to buy only dishwasher-proof items.

Pots and pans – the absolute minimum
One large saucepan and lid
One medium saucepan and lid
One small saucepan
One frying pan (non-stick)
One casserole dish and lid, preferably both oven and hob proof
Roasting trays
Grill pan

£100–£300

In this category, you will also need to provide an assortment of oven-to-table souffle, quiche, lasagne, pie and crumble dishes, either matching your tableware (see below) or in a style complementary to it. The numbers and sizes will depend on your maximum number of guests, but try to ensure that each dish is large enough to feed everyone at one sitting. If not, buy two identical ones. **£50–£150**

Knives

A surprising number of people cook properly on holiday (many say they enjoy it and do not have time at home). Therefore decent knives are something you may want to invest in. Looked after properly, and most guests will treat them with care, they will last indefinitely.

Sabatier is one good brand, but there are plenty of others on the market. Whatever you end up buying, make sure that either the blade is bolted through the handle or that the whole knife (handle and blade) is made out of a single piece of steel.

The knives you will need are:
Bread knife (serrated)
Carving knife
Carving fork
Large vegetable knife
Small vegetable knife
Knife steel

£50–£150

Kitchen miscellany
Small, medium and large Pyrex bowls
Sieve
Colander
Cheese grater
Corkscrew and bottle opener
Tin opener
Measuring jug (two, if the house sleeps more than six)
Trivets for hot dishes
Hand whisk
Wooden spoons (minimum of three and replace often)

Potato masher
Straining spoon
Ladle
Fish slice
Spatula
Serving spoons
Kitchen scales
Scissors
Ice-cream scoop
Tablespoon
Potato/vegetable peeler
Pastry brush
Garlic crusher
Salad bowl and pair of salad servers
Fruit bowl
Lemon squeezer
Cafetière
Tea caddy
Tea strainer
Small bowls for olives, dips, etc
Jug for fruit juice, water, etc
Bread bin
Butter dish
Salt and pepper set
At least two plastic chopping boards – one clearly marked for meat
Wooden bread board
Rolling pin
Toast rack
Tea towels
Oven gloves
Kitchen apron
Serving and place mats, coasters

Bin – Brabantia has a robust range which comes with its own bin liners. This may sound prissy, but it does look better if the liners fit neatly and do not spill out in a great ruff around the top

Dustpan and brush

Washing up bowl

Drainer

Fire extinguishers

Fire blanket

Torch

Plug adaptor

£550–£650

Optional kitchen items

Pestle and mortar

Nutcrackers

Vases for cut flowers

Spoon rests

Lemon zester

Electric whisk

Blender/liquidiser

Steamer

Wine rack

Egg cups

Egg timer

Ramekin dishes

Wine stoppers

Knife block

Steel and/or wooden barbeque skewers

Mandolin (slices vegetables very finely)

Empty storage jars

Cake tin

Cook books (guests use them a lot)

£250

Tableware

Do not ever buy the exact number of anything end-of-range because when something inevitably gets smashed or lost you will not be able to replace it. So either buy double the quantities you need or stay with a range you know will continue.

Crockery – the absolute minimum per person
One dinner plate
One side plate
One cereal bowl
One cup and saucer
One tea/coffee mug
And two spare of everything.

But that is rather sparse so try to provide perhaps four spares, plus pasta/soup bowls (the wide, shallow ones) and double up on the tea/coffee mugs. Apart from the mugs, this is one time when it is best to go for a matching set. It is difficult to put together an artistically mis-matched dinner service without it looking like a load of junk shop rejects, no matter how much it all cost. It is all down to taste and how much you want to spend, but something like the blue and white Denmark crockery is reasonably priced, goes with most styles, is dish washer safe, and sold everywhere so is easy to replace. **£150–£350**

While you are choosing crockery consider buying the following in the same range: not all of these are vital and they do not have to match, but frankly it is easier if they do because by this stage your appetite for picking tasteful items will be beginning to wane (and there is a long way to go yet).

Teapot
Vegetable serving dishes, possibly with lids
Milk jug
Cream jug
Sugar bowl
Gravy boat

£75–£150

Cutlery – the absolute minimum per person
One knife
One fork
One dessert spoon
One tea spoon
And two spare of everything.

Again, try to be a bit more generous because there is nothing
more irritating on holiday than constantly having to wash up just
to have a cup of tea.

For a property sleeping four provide eight to ten sets of cutlery;
for those sleeping six, 12–14 sets, and so on. The numbers will
depend on what sort of cutlery you buy because a lot comes in
pre-packaged sets. Bistro-style cutlery is a good all-rounder
because it is versatile and hard-wearing. But if you buy this then
make sure it is decent quality because there are some terrible
imitations around. Habitat does a good version. Do not buy
anything with wooden or bone handles because they are generally
not dishwasher-safe and should not be left to soak.   £20–£150

Glasses – the absolute minimum per person
One wine glass
One small tumbler (for fruit juice and spirits)

One large tumbler (for beer and soft drinks)
One medium plastic tumbler (for children/adults in the garden)
And two spare of everything.

Ideally, try to provide both red and white wine glasses. Again, if possible, it is probably best to go for decent quality matching sets. Michelangelo is a good brand of wine glass and is sold pretty much everywhere. **£30–£100**

Furnishing the rest of the house

Curtains, properly made and fully lined, and/or blinds
Curtain poles
Lampshades
Pictures (a minimum of two per room)
Telephones
Waste paper bins (one per room, preferably metal)
Smoke alarms
Carbon Monoxide detector
Vacuum cleaner
Broom
Mop
Bucket

£1,500 approx

Living room
TV, DVD/video player
TV table or equivalent
CD player
Coffee/occasional tables
Side/reading lamps
Cushions/throws
DVD/video cassettes. Family classics are safest, eg James Bond,

Hitchcock, Harry Potter, *The Lord of the Rings*, other Oscar
winners
Games/jigsaws/cards
Books
Local Ordnance Survey map (usually heavily used)
Visitor book
Candles
Fire guard
Coal scuttle
Log basket

£1,250–£2,000

Bedrooms
Wardrobes, if none are fitted
Chests of drawers/dressing tables
Mirrors
Hangers
Bedside tables
Bedside lights
Bedside clock/radios
Spare blankets
Hairdryers
Hooks for the backs of doors

£400–£1,000

Bathrooms
Bathroom cabinet or mirror
Towel rails
Loo roll holder
Loo brush and holder
Soap dish/dispenser
Bath mats
Hand towels

Shaving adaptor plug (if no socket available)
Pedal bin

£150

Laundry
Iron and ironing board
Laundry basket (clean wet clothes)
Linen basket (dirty clothes)
Clothes airer
Pegs

£100

Babies/young children
High chair
Cot
Stairgate
Selection of melamine/plastic bowls, plates, cups
Cutlery

£150–£200

Outside
Garden furniture: table and chairs, deckchairs (definitely nothing
   plastic, teak or the equivalent is best)
Barbeque
Washing line
Dustbins (minimum two, and at least three if you accept six or more
   guests)

£200–£300

STOCKISTS

It is difficult not to sound like a free advertisement for anyone,
but John Lewis carries many things you will need. Habitat is
particularly strong on beds and bedding. IKEA is excellent for

cheap, robust tumblers, ice cube trays, mugs, wine stoppers, and on storage items. Homebase is also strong on kitchenware, as is Lakeland. Argos stocks particularly good value duvets and pillows.

THE GARDEN

This book is not the place to advise on garden design (or this author the person to do it). But remember that whatever you do outside, it has to be robust enough to stand up to children's ball games but still be pretty enough for guests to want to sit in. If you intend to let the full 12 months, it also needs to have year-round appeal. Unfortunately, the garden also has to be easily maintained, preferably within the short period of time you have on each changeover day.

These factors limit what you can do, so either get a gardener or plant lots of evergreen shrubs (the ones that keep their leaves all year round) and perennials (things that flower year after year with minimal input from you).

Aim to plant flowers and shrubs closely together and scatter bark between them to suppress weeds.

Pots and window boxes

These can dramatically brighten up a garden but they need watering regularly. Many guests, especially keen gardeners, are happy to do it because taking a watering can around a pretty garden on a summer's evening is not exactly a hardship, but you cannot rely on this. So:

- ◆ Make sure containers are as large as possible.
- ◆ Keep them in the shade to reduce water evaporation.

- Cover the soil around the plants to help it hold moisture (use bark, or pebbles and shells in seaside areas).
- Use slow release water-retaining gel or crystals.
- Consider mini irrigation systems which work on timers.

Geraniums are virtually indestructible and are probably worth a risk, even on a sunny doorstep, and particularly if you line a terracotta container with plastic to prevent evaporation. They are also thought to flower better under stress.

Realistically if it is a small, mature garden then you or your housekeeper should have time to mow the lawn and keep on top of the weeding. But if the garden is newly planted, fiddly or larger, then you may have to employ a gardener anyway.

Decking, gravel and paved patios
If all else fails then the ultimate low maintenance solution for small gardens or courtyards is to take up the lawn and cover the whole lot with one of the above. Remember though that they are not as child friendly, and some patios and decking can become slippery when wet, especially under trees.

If you decide on gravel then prepare the ground carefully first, otherwise you will spend the next ten years regretting it. This means digging a drain if it is a boggy area, micro weeding, laying a water-permeable but weed-proof membrane, and only then spreading a minimum two or three inch layer of gravel.

When weighing up the pros and cons, remember also that paved areas and decking can be swept clean and fallen leaves easily removed. It is far more difficult to do this on gravel.

8

Cleaning a Holiday Cottage

B y now you will probably have decided whether to clean the property yourself or employ a housekeeper. Regardless of who does it, the property has to be spotless, cleaner than you ever thought possible, and certainly far cleaner than the average family home. Guests will not tolerate anything less than perfection (or the closest you can get to it) and they will be quick to complain if is not.

So that means not just regular vacuuming and dusting, but also ensuring no sticky food cupboards or fridges, no hairs in the bath plughole, no fluff under the beds or sofas, no cobwebs, no splattered mirrors: in short, showroom conditions. But the big consolation is that regular weekly cleaning really does work. It is far easier to keep a clean house clean than start from scratch on an untidy and dirty one.

Even if you employ a housekeeper and live a long way away, at least consider helping with the occasional changeover. There are four good reasons for this:

1. You learn how people use the property: what they do, where they sit, what and how they eat and how well they look after it. All this information is useful in assessing whether the furnishings and housekeeping are adequate. It is also useful if you are considering buying other investment properties in the future.

2. You can assess the rate of wear and tear.

3. You can decide where, if any, there are savings to be made or whether you have to increase your spending in order to justify rent levels.

4. You can keep a personal eye on your investment and check on the levels of service you are receiving from your housekeeper and gardener.

THE IMPORTANCE OF A ROUTINE

It is essential to have a routine otherwise the cleaning will not be finished in time.

Speed and efficiency

It is far better for the same person to clean the property each week. The maximum time between guests is probably six hours, but is more likely to be four or five. This means the system has to be a model of streamlined efficiency, a text book study in time and motion, which allows you to sweep effortlessly through the house without having to constantly go back and retrieve the vacuum cleaner. It will take a surprisingly long time to refine a system: it will not be perfect after a couple of weeks but after perhaps 10 or 12 weeks life will begin to get easier.

Checking and replacing

Going through the same tasks in the same order week after week is a foolproof way of checking nothing has been broken or chipped, lost or stolen. So even if the property is spotless, if the guests have stayed only a couple of nights, or the outgoing guests tell you they have done the cleaning themselves (and a surprising number will), *still* clean and put everything back in its place. And after a few weeks of doing that, anything wrong or missing will stand out a mile. Looking around the room, no matter how thoroughly, is not the same and does not work.

Allowing for disasters and extra jobs

Remember this is cleaning with a deadline: it is not the same as employing a daily or weekly cleaner for your own home where jobs can be picked up and finished off when there is time. A good routine allows time for unexpected disasters (juice stains on carpets, broken video recorders), plus time for extra tasks which will not need doing every week.

A RECOMMENDED SYSTEM

Anyone who has ever cleaned a house will have their own thoughts and methods, but this system has worked well for me and it will at the very least provide you or your housekeeper with a starting point for those first few scary weeks.

What you will need

First, buy three or four plastic boxes of the type sold in virtually every DIY, hardware store or supermarket. They do not need to be enormous, something about 12 inches wide and slightly longer, but they do have to be robust.

◆ In box one, keep the items you will need each changeover day. These will probably include rubber gloves, a duster and furniture polish, bathroom and kitchen cleaner (you will probably want both because kitchen cleaners are better at getting rid of grease), cloths, liners for inside and outside bins, disposal bags for nappies and sanitary items (critical in rural areas with septic tanks), screwdriver, both cross-head and slot (a surprising number of things need tightening and it is easier to do as you go around), a stain remover like Vanish for tackling marks on carpets and upholstery, and dishwasher tablets. Keep loo rolls and soap in this box too.

◆ In box two, keep spares of the above plus other materials you will not use as often, for example window cleaner. Also in this box keep spares of cleaning materials you leave for the guests. This will probably include washing up liquid, loo cleaner, kitchen and bathroom cleaners. You need to keep spares of everything in the house because you will not have time on changeover day to go out and buy more.

◆ In box three, keep spares of small household items, light bulbs, matches, pegs, potato or vegetable peelers, tin and bottle openers and extra cutlery. Items go missing, especially bottle openers during the picnic season, and other items quickly become tarnished or dirty (like tin openers). It is easier to buy those cheaply and replace frequently, rather than buying decent quality and spending precious minutes on changeover days trying to clean them.

◆ In box four, keep crockery replacements. The majority of guests will not break anything: occasionally you get an accident prone family, but this is rare. If you are experiencing breakages regularly, then look closely at your dishwasher, the position of the taps in relation to your kitchen sink or the type of guests you are attracting.

You can never have too many boxes. You may want another for replacement food, ie tea, coffee, sugar, biscuits, salt and pepper, but the size and importance of this box will obviously be decided by what supplies, if any, you decide to leave your guests.

Where to keep your boxes

Obviously the best place is at the property, preferably in a discreet and lockable cupboard. It is best if the cupboard is locked because guests can be inquisitive, but at the same time not want to be reminded of the mechanics behind their holiday. Clearly it is also far better to keep your cleaning fluids and other potential hazards away from guests' small children.

THE CLEANING

This will depend on the lay-out of the property, number of bathrooms, whether you do the garden and how many hours you have, but it should go something like this:

Hour one

On changeover day arrive at the house five minutes after the time the guests should have left. If you can see they have left early then go in immediately because you may need all the time you can get. Some guests like to linger on the last morning for a relaxed chat. They will talk about where they have been, and in seaside areas children will present pebble collections. But you have to be ruthless, so politely but firmly steer them out with tales of terrible traffic building later in the morning.

Once they have gone immediately open the windows. All families leave their scents behind. It could be dog, perfume, cigarettes, children, cooking, whatever, but remember that you will only have a few hours to disperse it. Use air freshener only as a last resort because the chemicals linger, and it will be obvious if you have used a masking agent.

Go into the kitchen. Arrange fresh flowers in water and throw out the old ones. Open oven doors and check for spillages. If really bad, put oven cleaner on now. Also check the microwave, dishwasher, washing machine, tumble dryer, bread bin and so on, leaving all the doors open. Check the fridge and freezer and oven hob. Again, any disasters are easy to treat if they picked up early. While you are doing this have a general look around. You will quickly learn to tell if you are in for an easy or nightmare few hours.

The orthodox approach is to clean a house from the top downwards, but it does not make any difference. Instead, start with an area of the house which can be finished quickly so that if guests do want to drop luggage off early they can do so. This could be a bedroom or entrance hall or living room.

Starting with bedrooms, strip all the beds on one floor. As you go, put the bedding in a bin liner. Also remove bath mats and towels. Get the bin liner out of the way immediately: put it in your car, in the hall or wherever. Roll the top down so the contents are visible. This way you do not accidentally empty the bins into it or throw it out with the other rubbish.

Aim to turn mattresses once a month. New mattresses should be turned weekly for the first three months or so, both end-to-end and side-over-side. Remember which ones you have done by doing a mattress a week and always in the same room order. At the same time as turning the mattress, wash its cover and the pillow protectors. Make up the beds.

Get a duster and tin of furniture polish. Work around each room, ending by the door. Dust and polish surfaces, turn lights on and off to check bulbs, draw curtains to check they haven't dropped off hooks, wipe off smudges from light switches and socket points. Check smoke and carbon monoxide detectors. Also check the time is set correctly on bedside clocks and the radio is tuned to something (anything). Check as well wardrobes, cupboards, drawers, under the bed, and most importantly of all, the hooks on the backs of doors because this is where most things are left. Send on all items.

Clean all bedrooms on the same floor in turn. Do the connecting hall or landing. Vacuum all the rooms together and that is one section finished. Assuming there are no disasters, it should take 15–20 minutes a bedroom.

Hours two and three

Depending on the layout of the property, it may be easier to clean bathrooms together after the bedrooms are finished. Then you do not have to constantly switch between duster, polish and vacuum cleaner, and cloth, cream cleaner and mop.

Start with the bath or shower area. Spray the tiles lightly with cleaner and wipe off with a damp cloth. If you are lucky enough to live in a soft water area, then a squirt per wall will be enough. Hard water areas leave far more water marks so it is important not to let it get too bad in the first place. Instead, encourage guests to spray the area after showering with something like Mr Muscle shower shine which does seem to work. Clean the bath, shower spray and/or shower screen, again with a minimum of cleaner. Pay particular attention to the plughole, removing all trapped hair, and around the taps.

After cleaning the bath and shower screen, wipe them with a tea towel or similar so they dry more quickly and with fewer water marks. Dry, clean surfaces look better than wet, clean ones.

Clean the inside and outside of the loo pan and under the seat. Wipe the seat and around the hinges. Wipe the cistern. Pour down the pan a green or blue loo cleaner. Also:

◆ wipe any shelves, the inside of bathroom cabinets, and dado rails
◆ wipe down windows and sills
◆ dust extractor fans
◆ empty pedal bins and replace the liner
◆ throw away any used soap and other used toiletries
◆ wipe and dry mirror
◆ put out fresh soap and full roll of loo paper (plus a spare)
◆ refill or replace bottles of bubble bath/salts
◆ put out a fresh hand towel and bath mat
◆ leave an adequate supply of loo and bath/shower cleaner, disposal bags for sanitary material and nappies, shaving adaptor plug, and clean cloth for wiping out the bath (make sure it is clean: nothing is more revolting than a grey and greasy rag).

Clean the wash basin, taps and surround, and wipe dry. Finally, vacuum or sweep the floor and wash it.

Tackle stairs and landings as you go. There is no particular trick to these, apart from vacuuming or brushing stairs thoroughly because they take so much punishment, and looking closely at the high ceilings above stairwells for cobwebs, spiders, dead moths and flies, and other things that lurk out of the way.

Hours four and five

By now, a significant amount of the cleaning should be finished.
Over the weeks you or your housekeeper will learn to judge
progress by time or whatever is on the radio at a given point
(Radio 4 on Saturday mornings (the most common changeover
day) is conveniently divided into 30 minute sections. If they are
on to *Any Questions* and you are still doing your first room, you
know you are in trouble.) So in the early days, while a routine is
still being established, stick to mini deadlines.

Turn your attention now to the reception rooms. On the whole
these are the easiest to do because there is no tricky wet cleaning
and no beds to change.

As with the bedrooms, work your way methodically around the
room, checking lights and curtains, dusting surfaces, wiping
coasters and light switches, re-arranging furniture, emptying
waste paper bins and tidying away books, games and videos
which may have been left out.

Pull cushions off chairs and sofas and vacuum underneath. Often
you find something: usually knitting needles, sweet wrappers,
loose change, orange peel, remote controls, bits of Lego. The
same applies to under sofas and easy chairs: pull them out, rescue
the object, give the carpet a good vacuum and shove it all back.
Check under rugs as well. Clean out any open fires or wood
stoves, sweep hearths and grates, and replenish stocks of wood
and coal. Vacuum everywhere and exceptionally thoroughly under
dining tables.

Finally, to the kitchen. You or your housekeeper may prefer to do
this first, but if you leave it to the end it gives any oven cleaner

the maximum time to work and allows white goods to 'air' for as long as possible with their doors open.

Method is especially critical here because the kitchen, along with the bathroom, is where you will be most closely judged, and where guests will be quickest to complain if anything is wrong.

So start somewhere logical and do everything in a vertical sweep, for example the wall mounted cupboard, the microwave on the work top beneath it and the tumble dryer in the cupboard under that. Then move onto the next section and so on. Wipe clean the work surfaces and cooker hob at the end.

The fridge and freezer should not be too much of a problem: sweeping out crumbs and wiping everything down is usually enough. Check the soap drawer in the washing machine has not become clogged with powder detergent. Clean the filter in the tumbler dryer if there is one. Also have a look at the filter in the dishwasher: it is not uncommon to find whole sprouts, cheesy crusts or the odd teaspoon wedged in it. Empty the bin and wash inside and under the lid.

Not surprisingly, by far the worst problem is usually the ovens. The top oven is often particularly bad after families with young children have stayed because of the open grilling of sausages, burgers and fish fingers. At the other extreme, with the main oven, couples who at home do not cook a roast from one year to the next go on holiday and have three in a week.

Allow time to scrub oven shelves, grill and roasting trays in order to keep on top of the problem. Putting them through the dishwasher will help if the grease is recent, but if it has been caked on by repeated use through the week then it will only make matters worse. One way to minimise the problem, at least with the trays, is to leave them lined with fresh foil and hope guests take the hint. Also consider bulk buying the turkey trays that many supermarkets now sell in the run up to Christmas. They cost less than £1 each, and will only last a limited time, but you may decide it is better to buy cheap and replace often then waste valuable time on changeover days trying in vain to clean up your existing trays.

Leave an adequate supply of washing-up liquid, dishwasher tablets, rinse aid, salt, oven cleaner, kitchen cleaner, and stain remover. Leave a supply of bin liners, both fitted for the inside kitchen bin and large black ones for outside.

If you have decent knives, sharpen them with the steel. It will only take a couple of minutes and is worth it.

LESS FREQUENT JOBS

These do not need doing every week, but if you or your housekeeper have time, try to complete at least one each changeover day.

- cleaning windows, inside and out
- dusting beams
- dusting the tops of cupboards
- dusting banisters and between uprights
- dusting the tops of pictures
- removing books from shelves and cleaning behind them
- touching up paint work.

FORTNIGHT VISITORS

If your guests stay longer than a week you have to decide whether to clean mid way through their stay. If you let through an agency it may well have its own policy, otherwise consider these points:

Against

◆ It is not wise to go unaccompanied into the property during a holiday, so either make sure the guests will be there or take a friend.

◆ Be aware you will have to clean around guests' personal possessions, possibly moving dirty washing or valuables in order to do so.

◆ Some guests prefer to be left alone, either because they value their privacy or because they feel obliged to tidy up beforehand.

In favour

◆ Some guests will expect it.

◆ The property will probably be untidier if it has been left for a fortnight rather than a week.

◆ In summer it is unlikely the garden can be left untouched for a fortnight, especially if there is a lawn, so you may have to go there anyway.

◆ If the guests are at the property, consider it a good opportunity for customer care and feedback.

If you decide not to clean half way through the guests' stay, the bedding, hand towels, bath mat and tea towels will still have to be changed after a week. So in advance of a fortnight booking, prepare double sets of everything. When the guests arrive, offer them *gracefully* the choice of changing their own beds or you returning to do it. Nine times out of ten they will say they prefer to do it themselves.

9

Managing a Holiday Cottage

U nless you hand over complete control of your property to an
agency, you will at some stage meet your guests. There is an
argument for meeting a cross section anyway: it helps you fine tune the
service you are offering (in the same way as doing the occasional
changeover can); it is useful market research; and personal contact can
minimise complaints, if you ever get any.

How to meet your guests can be tricky. I am not suggesting you
invite yourself around for dinner: instead, you could be there to
welcome them on their arrival; phone them a day or two after
they have settled in; or perhaps drop in for five minutes if it is an
informal type of set up. Do not fire off questions from a prepared
list: it is enough to ask if they are enjoying their holiday and to
check they have everything they need.

MERITS OF A PERSONAL WELCOME

Some agencies encourage owners or housekeepers to greet guests personally. Logistically this is easier if you live close by, in the neighbouring farmhouse for example, otherwise guests have to notify you in advance of their estimated arrival time but may not want to be held to it on the day.

Many guests do appreciate the personal contact and it is by far the best way to hand over keys and explain about any house quirks. It is also a good chance to impress on guests that they can phone at any time with queries, though strangely hardly any ever do. And if anything does go wrong, guests are less likely to go off at the deep end if they have met the person on the other end of the phone.

But there are plenty of other guests who may have had a long and stressful drive, and are horrified at having to make polite conversation with a complete stranger. They cannot wait to get rid of you.

What is probably more important is that you or your housekeeper are available on the end of a phone for the first couple of hours after the guests have arrived to answer any questions which may arise.

WHAT GUESTS EXPECT ON ARRIVAL

- Clear, uncomplicated directions on how to find your property.

- Being able to park close to the cottage to unload. If this is a problem then guests should be warned before booking.

- A cast-iron method of getting the keys. The options are:
  – either you or a housekeeper meet the guests at the

property and hand over the keys personally

   – they are posted in advance to the guests

   – they are left outside in a key safe and the guests are sent the
     PIN in advance

   – they are left in a shed or outhouse

   – they are collected from a neighbour.

◆ No intricate or slipping locks to master.

◆ A heating and hot water system which is simple to use.

◆ Depending on the time of year and the system, the heating and
hot water are turned on in advance.

◆ Depending on the time of year, the property is left warm, cosy
and lit or cool and light with plenty of open windows (security
permitting).

◆ All beds have been made up, regardless of the number of
guests.

◆ A TV/satellite/DVD system which is quick and easy to use
(somewhere to park small children while they unpack).

A tea tray with fresh milk is also universally welcome, as is a
vase of fresh flowers.

OPTIONAL EXTRAS

◆ Consider offering a more generous tea tray: it is even better if
it reflects local specialities. In the West Country it could be a
cream tea. A scone per person, a bowl of jam (covered in cling
film) and some clotted cream costs barely more than a decent
packet of biscuits but the effect and therefore the welcome is
far better.

- Some owners provide a bottle of wine. This is a nice touch but the expense adds up over the year. And you have to ask yourself if guests who have paid hundreds of pounds to stay in your cottage will be happy with a bottle of the vinegar you have left over from your last Calais wine run. Something around the £5 mark is probably safe.

- One or two of the more expensive holiday letting agencies expect their owners to supply welcome hampers. Typical contents include bread, butter, eggs, cheese, marmalade, orange juice, biscuits and cake, plus some regional foods. Only do this if you are going for the top end of the market and the cost can be recouped in the higher rents you are able to charge.

- The decision on what to leave may be easier if you are a farmer or smallholder. A box of home-grown fruit or vegetables, home-baked bread, freshly laid eggs, or cheese or yoghurt from your own dairy is more personal than a hamper of glossy wrapped luxuries and rather more useful.

- Some owners of top-of-the-market properties supply baskets of complimentary toiletries. Again, only do this if you are charging enough to justify it.

- Some owners provide towelling bathrobes, but remember that these will need washing every week and will have to remain in pristine condition.

- If you know your guests have taken the holiday to mark a special occasion (honeymoon, landmark birthday, wedding anniversary, new job) consider leaving a bottle of champagne and chocolates. A surprising number of guests will mention the occasion when booking so ask your agency (if you are using one) to tip you off.

◆ At Christmas send cards to your guests who have holidayed with you that year, plus any other regular guests from the past. The cards will not persuade guests to return if they do not want to, but will at least remind them that you still exist.

◆ For Christmas and New Year bookings expect to supply a tastefully decorated tree (not too many gaudy plastic fairies), but check with the guests first. Remember that some people may not celebrate Christmas or they may have particular and personal reasons for wanting to be away from home at that time of year and not be reminded of the festivities.

FOOD

What to supply
The minimum is usually tea bags, milk and sugar, salt and pepper.

Some owners offer to shop for a starter pack of groceries to help guests through the first evening. This may be useful if the guests are expecting to arrive late but in practice, now that supermarkets are open virtually round the clock, this is not so necessary. If you decide to offer this service make sure you are either paid in advance or that there is some other method of recouping your money. There is nothing more embarrassing than on the last morning agonising about how to tactfully ask for your £20 back.

What to leave in the house
Many guests will leave food behind for the following week's visitors on the basis that a lettuce or pint of milk will not be at their peak after spending eight hours in a car boot on the way home. But very few guests will use anything, especially if it has already been opened. The exceptions are generally:

- tea, coffee, drinking chocolate and sugar
- herbs and spices
- olive or any other cooking oil (but make sure the bottle and cap are clean)
- occasionally rice, pasta and pulses, but only if they look newly opened.

Throw everything else away.

GUESTS' INFORMATION FOLDER
It is important to get this right for a number of reasons:

- The folder is one of the first things guests will turn to when they have brought their bags in and are sitting down with a cup of tea/glass of wine. Rips, stains and spelling mistakes do not add up to a great first impression.

- Comprehensive household information should stop guests phoning you in the middle of the night to find out how to switch on the heating.

- Well-written and informative tips on the best beaches, favourite shops, walks, golf courses, etc, go down particularly well. Guests frequently comment on suggestions left in the folder. It is even better if you include places which are off the beaten track and where other visitors do not usually go.

What to include – household information
- A note of welcome.

- The address and contact numbers of either you or your housekeeper.

- The phone number of the cottage (if there is one) and

confirmation if it takes incoming calls. Where the phone directories are kept.

- Directions to the nearest public pay phone (in many rural areas mobile signals are still poor).

- Phone numbers and addresses for a doctor, dentist, nearest large hospital, police station and vet.

- Easy-to-follow instructions on how the heating and hot water systems work. Leave the manufacturer's guide too. Also include any tips on how to ensure a long, hot bath (leave half an hour for the water to heat up, run hot tap slowly). Guests love staying in old properties but sometimes do not appreciate the plumbing that goes with them.

- Any special instructions for the loo. If your rural cottage has a septic tank it is important to restrict what is flushed away.

- Easy-to-follow instructions on how to light wood stoves.

- Details of where the fusebox and stopcock are.

- Details of where the fire extinguishers and fire blanket are kept.

- Where to park, who not to block in and any local restrictions.

- Any particular security arrangements.

- Details of bin day and what facilities there are (if any) for recycling.

- Which chopping boards to use for meat, vegetables and bread.

- How to clean the tumble dryer filter (vital if the guests have young children because they will probably use it a lot).

- A plea for guests to water the plants if the garden is looking particularly dry (this is not as outrageous as it sounds: most people are happy to do this, especially since they benefit and if it avoids a visit from you).

What to include – local facilities
- Where the nearest local shops are.
- Where the nearest supermarket is.
- Where the nearest Post Office is.
- If milk is delivered.
- If there are any farm shops nearby.
- Where the nearest pub/restaurant is.
- Whether it is child friendly.

What to include – local attractions
This is your chance to write lyrically about your area. Sell it to your guests. Send them where no other tourist goes; tell them how to avoid the worst of the traffic; where to park to avoid paying; about the fisherman who sells his catch off the side of his boat; the best place to buy good local pictures direct from the artist; your favourite restaurant; the quietest beach; where to go at dawn to catch the sunrise and at dusk for the sunset.

What to include – inventory
A proper inventory will take you hours to compile accurately and it is doubtful if anyone will ever look at it again. However you have to provide one if only to protect yourself if anything goes missing. Try to remember to update it as the contents of your property change (as they undoubtedly will over the years) and console yourself with the thought that at least you only have to do it properly once.

ADDITIONAL SERVICES TO OFFER

Depending on the type of holiday cottage you decide to invest in, you may want to consider providing extra facilities and/or services.

- Bicycles. Either invest in them yourselves or do a deal with a local hire shop.

- Walking/horse-riding. Suggest routes for guests and if necessary arrange pick-ups and collections via local taxis.

- Farm tours. If your letting property is part of one, allow guests to look around. Many guests (especially those who are city-based) are fascinated by the intricacies of milking or what sheep do all day.

- Garden tours. If your cottage is in a region renowned for its gardens and many of your guests are likely to be keen garden visitors, try to arrange special visiting rights (small discounts, access out-of-hours) on their behalf.

- Sailing/canoeing. In popular sailing areas consider offering an advance booking service with a local hire company or sailing school.

If you do any of the above, talk first to your insurance company to check you are covered and will not assume any sort of liability if something goes wrong.

WHAT GUESTS EXPECT DURING THEIR HOLIDAY

Above all, as with a tenant in a long let property, guests want everything to work, easily and efficiently.

Even with a meticulous owner or careful guest, things will occasionally still go wrong. What is important is that you, the owner, took all reasonable steps to stop it happening in the first place, and if something does happen, then you resolve matters quickly.

It is common sense which will decide how quickly you have to react.

♦ Gas or oil leaks, bad fumes, burst pipes or continually tripping electricity fuses clearly demand immediate attention. It is useful to keep convenient a list of plumbers and electricians whom you can call at any time.

♦ Broken showers, smashed windows, damaged locks or any hazard that guests can trip over, should be dealt with on the day if possible.

♦ Most other things can be left until changeover day.

And do not overlook the small things which if not fixed can be irritating, so check:

♦ all light bulbs work
♦ all fuses
♦ all clocks and timers are set correctly (boiler, cooker, video, bedside clock radios)
♦ TVs, radios and videos are tuned in
♦ there are no showers which only dribble out cold water
♦ there are no radiators which never get warm
♦ loos always flush properly
♦ there are locks that lock and bolts that bolt.

None of the above is exactly unreasonable but there are still properties around which fail to deliver. Really the choice is up to you: if you want to holiday let and maximise your income, then you also have to spend time and money sorting out the niggles. Otherwise you risk your guests not returning and not recommending your property to their family and friends.

Guests' privacy

Apart from emergency maintenance leave your guests alone unless they approach you. Remember that they have chosen a self-catering holiday and many people do that because of the privacy it provides.

When you first start holiday letting it can be tempting to phone your guests every five minutes to check they are enjoying themselves and that they have everything they need. Resist this urge. After a while you appreciate that silence from your guests is a Good Thing.

Provide them with everything you think they may want, stress they can call you at any time, not just for problems but for help and advice too, and sit back and let them get on with it.

WHO PAYS FOR BREAKAGES?

This will probably depend on how much you are charging and where in the market your cottage is positioned. At the luxury or top end of the market, when guests are paying hundreds or even thousands of pounds a week to stay in your property, it looks rather petty if you try to charge them for every broken wine glass. Assuming the breakages are accidental rather than malicious, it is better to absorb the losses yourself. In practice, in a well-designed holiday cottage, there should not be many anyway.

If your cottage is closer to the bargain end of the market, and your guests are paying relatively little, there is probably a stronger argument for expecting them to cover the losses. The best way is to leave a note in the household information folder asking people to leave an amount to cover breakages or damage. Realistically if they do not, there is not much you can do anyway. The other way to tackle this is to ask guests for a small bond or deposit which is returnable after the property has been checked, but again this is not really ideal in the mid to top range of the market.

If damage is more serious then it will probably be an insurance claim.

WHO DOES THE CLEANING?

If you live near your holiday cottage you will have to decide if you want to clean on changeover days and manage the housekeeping yourself. Owner/housekeepers probably take more care of the property if only because they have a vested interest, but you may live too far away or decide that even if you do live locally you do not want to commit a day a week to cleaning.

If that is the case then you have to find a housekeeper. If you do not know of anyone personally then investigate cleaning agencies. In holiday areas you will often find agencies with much experience of cleaning holiday cottages and the process should be relatively straightforward. If not, it is probably best to seek advice from your holiday letting agency, and if necessary arrange some training for the housekeeper.

If you employ a cleaner/housekeeper, then make sure that if you are not on the end of a phone they have a list of electricians, plumbers, builders and odd job men and the authority to call them in the event of an emergency.

CLOSING DOWN FOR WINTER

You will have to decide whether it is worth letting in the winter. Christmas and New Year weeks are lucrative (usually about the same or only slightly less than you can charge in July and August) but prices drop right away between about the middle of November and end of February, depending on your area.

You may decide that the cost of keeping the heating on for guests and clearing up after them (all that mud) does not justify the rent you can charge. On the other hand, the property cannot be left empty and unheated for several months unless you properly mothball it, drain down the system and make it completely secure. If you are thinking about this, then talk to your insurance company first.

The third option may be to 'winter let' your property: this is where the property is holiday let, probably between April and October, and then let on a six-month tenancy for the rest of the time.

Most insurance companies will probably prefer your property is occupied as much as possible.

WHAT TO BAN

This is a tricky one. As far as protecting your holiday cottage is concerned, the ideal guest is fanatically tidy, childless, non-smoking, a non-red wine and coffee drinker, who does not have a dog and who is always out. Unfortunately this is rare so you have to decide what is acceptable to you personally and practically. It is tempting to ban absolutely everything, but be aware there are at least two problems with this:

◆ It does not look good in a brochure if the forbidden list is longer than the property description.

◆ If you do ban anything you are automatically restricting the number of potential guests.

Think about the following options:

Smoking

Fewer people smoke now so this is not such a big issue. If you decide to allow smoking then make sure it is confined to the reception rooms (definitely not the kitchen or bedrooms). You may decide to allow cigarettes but ban smellier cigars or pipes. Despite what you may think, it is possible to get rid of the smell of cigarette smoke in the five or six hours on changeover day. Be aware that if you allow smoking you may attract a disproportionate number of smokers.

Big dogs

Despite what doting owners say, big dogs definitely have the potential to create more damage and more mess than small or lap dogs. This is especially true in autumn and winter when there is not a big dog alive that does not enjoy rolling in a stream or muddy field.

Any dogs

There is always a risk of muddy paws or uncontrollable chewing, even if the dog is smaller than a handbag. However, if you allow no dogs at all you are cutting yourself off from a sizeable number of potential guests, especially in good walking areas.

Babies
It is difficult to justify discriminating against babies because on the whole tiny ones do not create much mess (assuming they are fed on and over a wipe-clean surface).

Children
Children are clearly more mobile than babies and therefore potentially more destructive (think small unguided missile). Tempting though it may be to ban them outright, this will again dramatically restrict your number of potential guests. If you are that concerned about furniture or ornaments, they probably should not be there in the first place.

However the situation on banning or restricting younger children is different if there are safety issues: this could be anything from ponds or streams in the garden to a cliff-top location, swimming pool or insecure balcony area. If in doubt seek advice and *always* err on the side of caution when setting a minimum age limit.

Outdoor shoes inside
Why are so many people surprised or affronted if they are asked to take off their shoes inside? Who wants mud, leaves and other debris trodden into their pile carpets? Please support my campaign to make it socially more acceptable to leave your outdoor shoes in the hall.

10

Buying for Student Children

P ush all thoughts of squalid student flats to the back of your mind. Today's students are increasingly likely to live in comparative comfort, thanks to the hugely popular trend of parents buying them houses or flats.

There are two main benefits. First, you can make sure your son or daughter is living in a safe property in a not-too-awful area, where the boiler and other appliances have been regularly maintained and serviced. And secondly, with luck, it could still prove to be a decent long-term investment.

There are several ways of achieving this, but the net result is usually the same. Your son or daughter lives in the house or flat rent-free, while the rent paid by his or her flatmates could either cover a mortgage or top up your child's income on top of the student loan. There is also the possibility of making some money if the property has risen in value by the time it is sold. And all this could be done by using equity from your family home that would otherwise have been sitting there doing nothing.

The sums could work like this:

◆ Assume three letting rooms at £50 per week each, equivalent to £600 every four weeks.

◆ That is £7,800 a year, divided by 12, equivalent to £650 a month (mortgage payments being calculated on calendar months).

◆ £650 a month buys you a £156,000 interest-only mortgage at five per cent.

When doing your own calculations, remember that there may be less rent due during the long summer holidays when the students are away and when discounts for this period are frequently negotiated.

What is critical is the ratio between property prices and typical rents. In increasing parts of the country the sums may simply not add up. In cities like London, Bristol, Oxford and Cambridge property is expensive, and the rent you would need to ask to cover the mortgage may not be achievable. Have a look at www.accommodationforstudents.com which will give you an idea of what is available across the country and the typical rents being charged.

Also be aware that the numbers of parents buying for student children have in some areas saturated the market and sent prices soaring. This is not necessarily a problem as long as you have realistic aims to cover most of your costs and provide somewhere for your son or daughter to live. Just do not assume double digit yields and galloping capital growth because those days are over.

HOW TO RAISE THE MONEY

Using your existing family home

One of the most painless ways to find the money for a student property is to raise money against the family home. After a few years of astounding growth in house prices, an average family may well have built up a significant amount of equity (the value of the property now, minus any remaining mortgage). You should have little trouble in arranging to borrow against your home in these circumstances, especially if you decide to stay with your original lender and have a good track record with them.

If you raise the money for the letting property in this way, then the loan will be secured on your family home and your own mortgage payments will rise accordingly. You will have to demonstrate you have enough personal income to cover the increased mortgage payments because any projected income from the student letting property cannot be taken into account.

The fine detail will be decided by your own personal circumstances, but essentially it could end up looking like this:

- ◆ You, the parents, raise money against the family home.

- ◆ You either buy outright or can put down a sizeable deposit on the student letting property.

- ◆ Your mortgage payments on the family home will rise.

◆ But your son or daughter takes the rent from the letting property (while living free themselves).

◆ This means you do not have to pay them an allowance to top up their student loan.

It is even neater if your increased mortgage payments are approximately equal to what you would have been planning to pay your son or daughter as an allowance anyway. And of course, there is the added bonus that the letting property may rise in value, and bring in a profit when it is eventually sold. For the foreseeable future it is safer to assume any rise in profits will be modest and certainly not to be depended on, but a lot will depend on your timescale.

Buy to Let mortgage

If you decide not to use your family home to raise the money, or do not have enough spare equity, then your second choice is probably to take out a Buy to Let mortgage. The principal differences are that the loan would be secured on the student letting property and not your own home, and that the size of the mortgage would be determined by the rentable value of the property and not by the deposit you have available, although a reasonable deposit will be required in any event.

This can be a tricky calculation (explained in detail in Chapter 2) and often it is not easy to meet the lender's strict criteria. If you decide to go down this route, then it will be necessary to do the sums as early as possible to make sure it is achievable.

If you do not have enough spare cash for a deposit, you could combine the above two methods and consider extending your mortgage on the family home to raise the deposit, and then take out a Buy to Let mortgage to cover the balance.

Taking out a second mortgage

Some lenders will allow you to take out a second and separate standard mortgage to buy the letting property if a family member is going to live in it. You would have to show you have sufficient income to cover both mortgages.

The principal advantage of doing it this way is that you will probably be allowed to put down a smaller deposit (perhaps 10%) rather than having to satisfy the more onerous demands of a Buy to Let mortgage where larger deposits are often necessary. Few lenders offer this type of second mortgage, so it may be best to go through a broker to find a lender who is willing.

Using an inheritance or selling investments

If one of these options is open to you then potentially it is the most trouble-free method because you would be a cash buyer, with no increased mortgage payments to worry about. But your decision may well be affected by your attitude to risk, time scale, and any possible penalties for early encashment of investments, when deciding if your money is better off in property or in the stock market.

Ultimately, much will depend on your individual circumstances and your own tax position. It is best to take professional advice, especially in relation to tax, before deciding which option is best for you. And you may decide in the end that it may not be worth it, especially if the property market is flat and you do not have enough equity in the family home to buy the letting property outright.

WHAT TO BUY

Unlike other investment properties, you will probably have little say in where you buy because it will be decided by where your son or daughter goes to university. Wherever it turns out to be, realistically your choices will probably be between a flat conversion and a terraced house. Remember that a flat over a shop or other commercial premises is often difficult to get a mortgage on and therefore more difficult to re-sell. If you want to make life easy for yourself, it is probably best to avoid them.

Ideally, the kitchen should be large enough to eat in and there should be a separate living room. Any dining room can be used as another bedroom. Unless your son or daughter demands otherwise (and you are an indulgent parent) a high proportion of bathrooms to bedrooms is not vital.

The internet has transformed the search for the right property, making it far easier than it would have been only a decade or so ago. Virtually all the research can be done before leaving home, which means you only have to make the journey to view a shortlist of properties and perhaps then make a second visit to finalise the purchase.

When you begin house-hunting, it is probably best to start looking where the students already are because this is not the type of market to try to break new ground. Students stick together in packs; they like to be near their friends, ie other students; they usually want to be close to wherever they are studying (more time in bed in the mornings); they want pubs and clubs and life; they do not, on the whole, like suburbia.

So, questions to think about before starting out:

- Maximum price you are prepared to pay.
- Minimum number of bedrooms.
- Minimum number of bathrooms.
- House or flat?
- New or old?
- Conversion or purpose built?
- Close to university or college?
- Close to public transport?
- Close to shops?
- Close to pubs, clubs and cinemas?

Students often look for accommodation in pairs, so four bedrooms in total could be a good balance (perhaps a three-bedroomed property plus converted attic or dining room).

A garden is not on the list. You have to ask yourself how likely your student children and their friends are to cut the grass and at least try to remember not to throw old bikes in the flower beds. You may be lucky and have the one 18-year-old in a thousand who enjoys gardening: on the other hand you could be realistic and buy them something where the garden has already been concreted over. If you decide to do the concreting yourself, check first that it will not devalue the property. Gravelling or something else low maintenance may be a better compromise.

HOW TO FURNISH THE PROPERTY

A straw poll among parents who have already bought student letting properties said their children's standards and expectations of furnishings were surprisingly high. Most reported that the furniture and interior decoration survived remarkably well for the two or three years that the property was occupied (with boys apparently being more house proud than girls). They added that the better the property and furnishings provided in the first place, then the better they were looked after. (NB: Providing a property for your student son or daughter is probably not necessary for the first year they are at university because they usually live in halls of residence.)

The rules for furnishing property for students are largely the same as for any letting property, so that means:

◆ Neutral painted walls. The inevitable magnolia is as good as any. It brightens up rooms, especially in dark terraced houses, and is easy to touch up.

◆ Hard-wearing lino or tiles in the kitchen and bathroom and carpets everywhere else. Hessian-backed 100% wool carpets are only £7 or £8 a metre, and it will probably cost less than £1,000 to do a typical three/four-bedroomed terrace. Laminate flooring is increasingly popular because it is cheap, easy to lay, wipes clean and does not absorb the smell of cigarette smoke or cheap red wine.

◆ Robust kitchens and bathrooms. If the ones which come with the property are too disgusting, then rip them out and put in new ones. Many new kitchens and bathrooms are now good value (once you strip out all the unnecessary bits like fancy handles, integral wine racks and under-cupboard lighting strips), and the extra cost will be justified because it will almost certainly add to the value of the property.

◆ Solid, modern furniture. Anything upholstered, for example sofas, should be in darker colours. Much modern furniture is astonishingly good value. It will not last for ever or become a treasured antique, but that is not the point of it. Use it all for a few years, then chuck it out when it starts to sag and start again.

◆ Ideally each bedroom should also contain a desk and chair.

Apart from the white goods, you can buy the whole lot from Ikea. Other good places to try are Argos and Homebase.

Unfortunately, unless there is enough spare furniture lying around at the family home, then you are probably going to have to buy it. Because the furniture will not have to last as long as in a standard furnished letting property, you can do it more cheaply than the list in Chapter 6. Budget to spend between £4,000 and £5,000. Wherever the furniture comes from, it *has* to be fire- and flame-resistant and meet current safety standards.

WHO MANAGES THE PROPERTY

By far the best person to manage the property is your very own child, unlikely though it may sometimes seem. They are on the spot and the property may be in their name, which gives them an excellent vested interest in making sure it stays relatively clean and tidy, or at the very least, still standing.

Furthermore, they have probably moved in their close friends as flat mates (met through that first year in halls), and friends are less likely to wreck the place than a stranger found through a university noticeboard or website. But there is a downside to taking in friends as tenants: if they do something that is not acceptable (leaving the gas on all night or eating your food) then it is far more embarrassing to tackle them.

You may want to find a good local builder who can be trusted to sort out emergencies. This is particularly important because there will be no local letting agent to seek advice from, and there is only so much you can do on the end of the phone a couple of hundred miles away when water is pouring through the ceiling. You may also want to keep at home a copy of the local *Yellow Pages*. Then if your son or daughter is away and there is a problem, you can check the directory and get on the phone to someone immediately.

Collecting the rent
As far as the mechanics of collecting are concerned, it is better for standing orders to be set up so the rent is automatically transferred each month from the flat mates and into your son or daughter's account (or wherever else it is going). This avoids the potential embarrassment and difficulty of your child having to chase up the money.

Summer rent reductions
There are different ways of calculating this, and there may already be an accepted method in the town or city where your son or daughter decides to study. Otherwise the standard is for the flat mates to pay full rent for ten months a year, and then go on to half rent for the two summer months of July and August to secure their occupancy for the coming academic year.

In popular tourist areas, there may be a strong parental temptation to evict all the students for two months and earn some good money by holiday letting the property to visitors.

Contracts
The Tenancy Agreement should be between whoever is named on the deeds as owner of the property (either you as parents or your son or daughter) and their flatmates, named as tenants.

The correct way is for the flatmates to sign standard Assured Shorthold Tenancy Agreements or equivalent. These are discussed in Chapter 6. The Tenancy Agreement should confirm the rent arrangements. Be aware of any pitfalls associated with the new licensing of HMOs. Talk to your local authority if in doubt.

Insurance

Some, but not all, insurers cover properties bought for student letting. Typically, the parent will be responsible for the buildings insurance and contents cover for the furniture they have provided. The student occupants will be responsible for insuring their own personal possessions. There are policies available which are specifically designed for this purpose, and cover items like computers, bikes and so on.

Bills

It is usual for the utility accounts and TV licence to be in the name of your son or daughter and the quarterly bills to be split equally between all the occupants. You could consider having a key meter for the electricity installed, which is when the key is loaded with credit in advance. This can be done in a post office or local shop.

Council tax

Students do not pay council tax. If all the occupants of the property are students, then the whole property is exempt.

SECURITY

Student-occupied property can be particularly vulnerable to break-ins and burglaries. There are several potential reasons:

- The properties they occupy may be in the worst areas of inner cities with higher crime rates.

- Everyone thinks that students are loaded with electronic gadgets.

- The property is likely to be empty during holiday periods, especially over the long summer break.

- If your son or daughter is at all gregarious there will be people constantly coming and going, and unfamiliar faces walking in will not be spotted.

- Can they and all their flatmates be guaranteed to double or treble lock the front door and check all the windows *every time they go out?* Old, cautious, home-owners over 30 do, but students?

At least, as a parent, try to make sure the property has a sturdy front door and some decent locks on the windows.

Think about installing a burglar alarm. However it may just draw attention to the fact that there could be something inside worth stealing, especially if the property is in an area where alarms are not common. You also have to consider whether a student who has trouble keeping hold of a front door key is going to be capable of arming and disarming the alarm, especially at 4 a.m. coming home after a party.

By far the best solution is to be nice to the neighbours, especially if they are families, and hope they will keep an eye on the property when it is empty. Depending on the circumstances, it may even be worth giving them a small retainer, but certainly a large bunch of flowers or other gift when the students return in the autumn.

WHEN TO SELL THE PROPERTY

Many parents sell when their son or daughter graduates. But there are some factors which you may want to think about before making your final decision:

◆ what property prices are doing in the area at the time
◆ whether your child is likely to maintain any links with the town or city
◆ whether you need the money for anything else
◆ whether you have the appetite for letting to other students.

Depending on how you arrange ownership of the property and if your son or daughter is likely to stay in the area after graduating (very likely in London), you may decide to keep the property and let your child buy it from you over a period of time, essentially in instalments.

If you are thinking about keeping the property on for general letting, then consider how buoyant the local market is and how much demand there is likely to be for rented accommodation. Speak to your son or daughter's university before they graduate and find out if they maintain an active accommodation list.

Anywhere though with large universities and/or hospitals is probably a good bet, and if the town or city has decent transport links, especially with London, then so much the better. It means there is a better chance of the property rising in value in the long term, or at least holding its value.

TAX AND HOW TO PAY LESS OF IT

There are many variables and much will depend on your own circumstances, so seek professional advice if you are not sure. Here are some options:

Putting the property in your son or daughter's name

Probably the most tax efficient approach is to put the letting property in your son or daughter's name which then becomes (in the HM Revenue and Customs (HMRC) definition) their Principal Private Residence, assuming of course they own no other property.

The income earned from the property can then be covered under the 'Rent a Room' scheme, which allows anyone to earn up to almost £4,500 a year in rent, tax free, as long as they are letting rooms in their property that they are living in themselves. Anything over and above that limit can then be set against your son or daughter's personal allowance, which is another £4,900 a year (approximately). This means that your child can earn just over £9,000 a year, or about £180 a week, in rent before they start having to pay tax. (But remember that if they have a part time job, some of this personal allowance may already be accounted for.)

The beauty of this scheme is its simplicity: there are no business receipts to be collected and no accounts to be prepared and submitted to HMRC. The only reason your son or daughter would ever have to complete an annual tax return is if they exceed the limit and have something to declare.

Putting the property in your own name

The other principal way of handling this is to keep the property in your own name, receive the rent and then deduct all your allowable expenses, before being taxed on whatever profit remains. You would then prepare your accounts and submit them to HMRC in the usual way.

But because you probably already have a family home (your own Principal Private Residence), you may have to pay capital gains tax when you sell the letting property. Each person has an annual capital gains allowance. Any amount over that allowance is liable for the tax, and is calculated, crudely, on how long you have owned the property and how much it has risen in value in that time.

If you think capital gains tax could be a problem (and remember that the property has to increase by a lot to make the tax really hurt) then there are ways of mitigating it. For example, you could put the letting property in more than one name (perhaps two parents and two children) and benefit from the total of the four people's joint capital gains allowance, which is £34,000 at the time of writing. And there are other ways of helping reduce a capital gains liability, so speak to your accountant to check the best way for you.

But is there really much point in going down this route when your son or daughter can, with far less bother, take rent of £9,000 a year tax free and not have any capital gains tax to pay anyway? And if you are worried that they may, if the property is in their name, sell as soon as your back is turned and use the money to fund their gap year (or years), then speak to your solicitor about drawing up a legal agreement which means the property cannot be sold without your permission.

11

Rules, Regulations and Legalities

There are some aspects of property letting which are non-negotiable, and these mostly relate to safety. As a landlord you have legal obligations to your tenants or guests to ensure their safety. If you let through an agent, you are still responsible. If you ignore your obligations or are shown to be negligent in any way, you could be convicted of a criminal offence.

Legislation and recommendations are frequently amended and updated, so it is essential you take advice on the current position before you begin letting. Remember that you are doing it to protect your tenants or guests as well as yourself.

Much of this chapter deals with worst case scenarios, so do not be put off. Common sense goes a long way here: the law expects you to be reasonable and responsible, not super human.

Remember too that tenants have responsibilities: they cannot pass *everything* onto the landlord. Lord Denning once famously ruled that tenants had a responsibility to behave in a 'tenant-like manner', which means roughly that it is reasonable to expect them to do small jobs around the house. These could include changing the light bulbs, replacing a vacuum cleaner bag or unblocking a sink.

BEFORE YOU LET FOR THE FIRST TIME

If you have bought a *new property* then the appliances should have been installed to current standards. However, as landlord it is still your responsibility to check, so get the service engineers around if you have any doubts.

If you have bought an *older property*, remember that the appliances or wiring may have been installed when different, probably less stringent standards applied, so again get the service engineers around. Be prepared to replace some things which may still work but don't meet modern safety standards.

GAS

All gas appliances, including boilers, fires, flues, ovens and hobs should be fitted by a qualified CORGI (Council for Registered Gas Installers) engineer. As a landlord you have a duty to ensure fittings and flues are maintained in a safe condition. They should run smoothly and reliably. The appliances have to be serviced at least annually by a CORGI-registered engineer.

The engineer will provide you with a signed record confirming the service has been carried out, and you must give a copy of this record to your tenant or guest within 28 days, or to new tenants before they move in. You should keep the records for at least two years.

If there is any doubt in your mind that the appliances are not working correctly, or if a tenant or guest has a non-trivial complaint, then call out a CORGI engineer immediately. About 30 people a year die from carbon monoxide poisoning caused by gas appliances or flues which have not been properly fitted or maintained so it is not worth taking chances.

Some signs which may indicate a gas appliance is not working properly include:

- Yellow or orange flames (except from fuel-effect fires which display this colour flame).
- Soot or stains around the appliance.
- Pilot lights which frequently blow out.

Checklist – gas
- Ensure the appliances are installed by correctly qualified engineers.
- Never use a DIYer, no matter how competent.
- If you did not arrange for installation get the appliances checked out.
- Try to avoid buying appliances second hand: new is far safer.
- Have all the appliances serviced at least once a year.
- Leave a copy of the servicing record with your tenant or guest.
- Leave the manufacturer's instructions for the appliances with your tenant or guest.

www.corgi-gas-safety.com

OIL

The rules and regulations governing oil are not as stringent as those covering gas but as a landlord you still have a responsibility to ensure that everything is as safe as you can make it. Ignorance of good practice or carelessness is no defence if anything goes wrong.

Any installations or servicing should be carried out by a 'competent person' such as an OFTEC (the oil firing technical association)- registered engineer.

The rules may be strengthened again in the future which means:

◆ Oil-fired boilers and other appliances installed in the past may not meet current standards.

◆ Paying particular attention to the type of flue which ventilates the boiler or fire.

◆ Being prepared to have your oil-fired appliance inspected annually by a suitably qualified engineer.

◆ If you are not given one, asking the engineer for a written record confirming the inspection has been carried out. Leave a copy of this record with your tenant or guest.

As with gas, it is far safer to buy appliances new from a reputable source.

www.oftec.co.uk

SOLID FUEL STOVES/OPEN FIRES

Make sure the chimney is swept regularly and that the fire chamber or fire basket is sound and crack-free. Provide a suitable container for logs or coal.

VENTILATION: FLUES AND CHIMNEYS

Under no circumstances must any flue or chimney which is used
to vent or provide air to an appliance be blocked or obstructed.
If they are, there is the possibility of a build-up of potentially
lethal fumes.

Your engineer should check the ventilation and flues during the
annual (or more frequent) inspection but you must still be aware
throughout the year of the importance of ensuring the flues or
chimneys are kept open, and carry out your own checks if
necessary. If in any doubt get the engineer to check them again.

ELECTRICITY

Your primary responsibility as owner is to make sure that the
electricity supply, appliances, appliance leads and plugs are *safe,*
correctly wired and correctly fused. If you are worried about the
supply consult a qualified electrician. If you are worried about an
appliance, then remove it immediately.

Common sense tells you it is best to buy your Kite-marked
appliances new, in their original boxes, from reputable sources,
where you can be sure they meet the latest safety requirements.
Many electrical items are now so cheap they are virtually
disposable. What is the point of buying second hand or from a
market just to save the odd pound?

At the time of writing it is not a legal requirement for the
electricity supply in a rented house to be tested regularly.
However it is recommended that you test regularly anyway
because it is the only way to be absolutely sure of confirming that

the supply and appliances are *safe*.

By far the easiest way to cover yourself, and to show you took all reasonable measures, is to get around a reputable and qualified electrician to do what is called the PAT (Portable Appliance Testing) on items like kettles, toasters and irons. They will then leave a sticker on the appliance showing the date it was tested. Get them to check the mains wiring supply at the same time. It sounds like a lot of fuss but it will only take two or three hours for a small to average sized property and, barring anything wrong, that is it for another year. It will be even neater if you can wrap up any gas or oil checks on the same day and you will only have one anniversary a year to worry about, though this does not absolve you from continuing responsibility throughout the year to make sure that everything is maintained in good order.

Checklist – electricity

◆ Unless there is a good reason otherwise, buy only new electrical goods.

◆ Large electrical items, for example immersion heaters or cookers, should be installed by correctly qualified engineers.

◆ If an appliance shows any sign of not working correctly, replace it.

◆ If the lead on an appliance shows any signs of fraying, replace the appliance.

◆ Do not attempt to make DIY repairs on items. It is not worth it: throw them away.

◆ Leave manufacturer's instructions with the tenant or guest.

- Check all the appliances before the property is let or re-let.

- Keep a record to show you have fulfilled your duties as landlord.

UPHOLSTERED FURNITURE

All upholstered furniture you provide has to be fire and flame resistant. This is a legal requirement. Anything you buy new from a reputable source should comply with the latest legislation and will carry a permanent label to confirm this. If in doubt do not buy it. Be extremely careful when buying secondhand. Items covered by the legislation include:

- bed bases, headboards and mattresses
- futons
- pillows
- sofas and sofa beds
- loose or stretch coverings for furniture
- armchairs and dining chairs
- nursery furniture
- scatter cushions and seat pads
- garden furniture which may also be used in a house.

Antique furniture, carpets and curtains, bed clothes, duvets, pillow cases and sleeping bags have been excluded in the past. Check the current position before you begin letting.

GENERAL SAFETY: PROTECTING YOURSELF

Consumer protection law means that equipment supplied in rented accommodation has to be of the same standard as new equipment. What this means in practice is that everything works as if it were new. Critically you have to be seen to be fulfilling your obligations, especially if something goes wrong, which is why it is important to keep a written record of your inspections. Leave the manufacturer's instructions for use with the tenant or guest. Make sure the tenants know the instructions are there so they cannot claim ignorance if anything ever does happen.

As far as the wider safety picture is concerned, then it is down to common sense. Potential hazards like loose fitting stair carpets, bathroom floors which become slippery when wet or crumbling garden steps should be sorted out immediately in order to protect yourself from a possible claim for liability. In any event, make sure you carry adequate and relevant insurance.

SMOKE DETECTORS AND CARBON MONOXIDE DETECTORS
These are now both so cheap and easy to buy there is no excuse for not installing them. The batteries should be checked regularly.

FIRE EXTINGUISHERS AND FIRE BLANKETS
Different types of extinguishers are recommended for different areas of the house or flat. Talk to your local fire brigade. Make sure your tenant or guest knows they are there.

The authorities also recommend you should display a notice in the letting property saying something like this:

In the event of fire:
1. Raise the alarm and make sure everyone is out of the building.
2. Ring the fire service.
3. Tackle the fire (if you can, but do not take chances).

HOUSES IN MULTIPLE OCCUPATION (HMOs)

There are special rules covering Houses in Multiple Occupation or HMOs. These are usually properties which are let as bedsits or similar, and may have shared kitchens, bathrooms, and other communal areas such as the entrance and stairwells. The legislation is detailed and complex.

But essentially it means that some HMOs now have to be licensed – those with three or more storeys, five or more people and two or more households. That by no means confines licensing to local authorities or housing associations. It is possible for a largish Victorian or Edwardian villa, of the type found in many British towns and cities, to fall into this category. There is also other additional or selective licensing which could affect smaller HMOs in some areas. If, as a private landlord, you are determined to go down this route then seek specialist and professional advice from the beginning. Certainly one of your first calls should be to your local authority.

HMOs can produce disproportionately large incomes when compared to what the same property may make when let to a single family. For example, bedsits may achieve rentals of £250–£300 each per month and you may get between four and six in an average house. The same house, let as a whole, may only make £600–£800 a month in total.

But HMOs can be far more labour-intensive to manage and are probably not for the faint-hearted. You may in the end decide it is not for the novice property investor, if only because the returns may not justify the extra work you will have to put in.

PRIVATE WATER SUPPLIES

If your letting property is not connected to mains water (as some country cottages are not) then the supply will have to be tested regularly. Talk to your local authority. Make sure your tenant or guest knows in advance if this is the case.

FINES AND PRISON

This is grim but possible if you fail to fulfil your legal obligations and something goes badly wrong. Pleading ignorance of the law is not a defence. If the case goes to a Crown Court, the maximum penalty could be an unlimited fine and the possibility of imprisonment.

WHO TO CHECK YOUR OBLIGATIONS WITH

There is no shortage of government bodies, local councils, advisory groups, professional organisations and so on all queuing up and desperate to give you advice. In no particular order they include:

◆ Health and Safety Executive
◆ Council for Registered Gas Installers (CORGI)
◆ local authorities
◆ local trading standards office
◆ local fire service
◆ reputable letting agencies
◆ reputable holiday letting agencies.

Most information you need can be found on the internet, but always check the source and when it was last updated.

REMEMBERING YOUR OBLIGATIONS

It is easy to forget the exact date that a boiler has to be serviced by, when the septic tank is usually emptied or which month the chimney sweep is due. The easiest way to keep track of everything is to start a Calendar of Compliance which is just a grand way of describing a bit of paper listing the relevant dates which you have stuck to the kitchen wall. Half a day spent planning the year ahead now is far better than any nasty surprises cropping up later in the year (like an overflowing septic tank).

RISK ASSESSMENTS

These are now common in business, and are not as alarming or as complicated or time-consuming as they may sound. You may want to conduct your own.

A risk assessment is just a list of things that could be a risk, along with some notes on how you have tried to reduce those risks. Keep a copy to show you have thought of it and review the situation every year.

Some people may argue that a risk assessment is just another sign of the Nanny State. That may well be, but the purpose of this book is to help a landlord avoid potential pitfalls and not campaign for social change.

If anything ever goes wrong be under no illusion that you as landlord will have to be able to *prove* you have done everything you should have. So think of it as realism and protecting your own back.

PROPERTY COVENANTS OR OTHER RESTRICTIONS

It is vital you check to make sure your property is not covered by any restrictive covenant or any clause in a lease which may forbid you from either long letting or holiday letting.

Examples could include a block of residential flats where the lease prohibits owners from sub-letting, or perhaps a ban on holiday letting, found sometimes in developments such as the conversion of several barns grouped around a courtyard. In both these instances, bans are often imposed in order to maintain a sense of community among the permanent residents.

By far the easiest way to get around this is to make sure *before you buy* that your solicitor is aware of your intentions so he or she can make the appropriate checks.

Obviously situations change and you will want to keep all your options open. So if there is any ambiguity or any suggestion that you may be restricted in any way, it may be better in the long run to find another property.

THE AGENT'S CONTRACT WITH YOU

If you employ an agent, either for your long-letting property or your holiday cottage, you should have a formal written contract or agreement spelling out the terms and conditions.

Agents take these contracts seriously and so should you. To agents, contracts represent business and income (especially if they are self-employed), and many agents will not hesitate to act to protect their interests if they feel they have lost money or their professional reputation has suffered in any way.

Clearly all contracts will vary slightly but the core elements should be the same.

Long-letting contracts

The agent will usually undertake to:

- Find a suitable tenant for the property (NB: the contract will usually make it clear the agent will make all reasonable efforts to find a good tenant, but they will bear no responsibility or liability if the tenant defaults in any way).

- Prepare a Tenancy Agreement and inventory.

- Collect and hold a deposit.

- Collect gross rent, deduct commission of X amount, pass on net rent to the landlord and prepare regular accounts.

- Collect income tax due on the rent on behalf of HMRC (the old Inland Revenue) if the landlord is non-resident or working outside the UK.

- Visit the property (usually every quarter).

- Arrange for emergency repairs to be carried out up to a fixed sum (typically around £100). The cost will either be deduced from net rent or paid by the landlord direct.

- Only provide management services while the property is let. But most will agree to make check visits to empty properties for a small additional charge.

In return you, the owner, will usually undertake to:

- Authorise the agent to act for you for an initial fixed period, which can then be extended if both sides want to. At any point after the end of the fixed period, either party can end the agreement with a minimum of one month's notice.

- Instruct the agent on a sole agency basis.

- Inform the property's insurers that it is to be let.

- Inform any lender on the property that it is to be let (and obtain any necessary consents).

- Make sure that if the property is leased then sub-letting is allowed.

- Maintain the property in a good condition and repair any defects promptly.

- Allow the agent to carry out emergency repairs up to a fixed sum.

- Agree that the agent will not be liable for loss or damage caused by the tenant, nor for any defects or disrepair at the property which could not reasonably have been discovered.

- Indemnify the agent against any legal action taken by a tenant.

- Supply the agent with at least three sets of keys to the property.

Holiday letting contracts
The agent will usually undertake to:

- Provide advice on all aspects of holiday letting.

- Prepare property details and advertise accordingly.

- Handle inquiries, send out brochures, take bookings.

- Take in payment from the guests and forward it on to the owner (usually in two stages, deposit and then balance).

- Guarantee rent once the booking has been confirmed. This means that if the booking is subsequently cancelled for any reason you will still receive the money. (Not all agents offer this service.)

- Negotiate with guests if a property, for whatever reason, becomes unavailable or unsuitable for holiday letting.

- Consider taking legal action against guests for non-payment of rent or for any other breach of the booking conditions.

- Refuse to take further bookings from a specified guest if you, the owner, has requested it.

In return you will usually undertake to:

- Make sure the property meets the standards as specified by the agency.

- Make sure the property is vacant and ready for letting by the agreed date.

- Make sure the property is thoroughly cleaned between guests.

- Make sure the property is kept fit for holiday letting purposes throughout the letting period.

- Not make any major changes to the property throughout the letting period.

- Not to take lettings privately throughout the letting period without the agent's prior agreement.

- Make sure that if private lettings are taken, then the agency receives its standard commission on the rent charged.

◆ Agree that you and your family or friends may only occupy the property during the periods as specified by the agency (usually this is extremely limited during the peak weeks in July and August).

◆ Agree to insure the property and its contents for the purposes of holiday letting and that the agency should be indemnified (or protected) against all claims arising from the letting of the property.

◆ Agree to inform the agency if you move abroad and cease to be defined as a UK resident by HMRC. As with long letting, the holiday agency becomes legally responsible for collecting any tax payable on the rents due to you and will pass the taxes directly to HMRC.

If you fail to honour any of the above clauses, agents usually reserve the right to deduct any money owing or expenses incurred from the rents it holds on your behalf.

Selling the property

If you want to sell the property while it is still holiday let your contract with the agency will usually state that no 'For Sale' sign can be displayed on or near the property, and that viewings must be restricted to when the property is unoccupied and not booked by guests. The contract will often also stipulate that you cannot complete on the sale of the property until the agreement has expired or without prior permission from the agency.

Early termination of the contract

Be especially careful here because if for any reason you are unable to continue holiday letting and cannot honour the remainder of your contract, it could prove costly, especially if there are still bookings outstanding. You could be responsible for any or all of the following:

♦ Any compensation claims from guests unable to take their holiday.

♦ Any costs or administrative fees incurred by the agency in the guests being transferred to another property.

♦ Any difference in rents charged between the two properties (the guests are likely to be upgraded if a similarly-priced property cannot be found).

♦ The cost of a brochure entry which could run into hundreds of pounds.

♦ The loss of any commission on any bookings made but not transferred for any reason.

♦ The loss of any anticipated commission on bookings not actually made but reasonably expected (this is usually calculated as a percentage based on the previous year's booking history).

In the most extreme cases this could add up to a lot of money. However, if you have a good working relationship with your agency and there is a genuine reason for being unable to continue holiday letting (not just changing your mind) then many agencies will probably waive some or all of the above costs.

If you ever think you may be unable to continue letting, then talk to your agency immediately. That way you can at least limit any financial damage by taking no more bookings from that point.

INSURANCE

It is financial suicide not to carry suitable and adequate insurance cover. There is no point in not doing so anyway because specialist insurance for long lettings or holiday lettings will probably cost you only slightly more than a normal domestic policy, but with the added bonus that it is a deductible expense and will therefore help reduce your eventual tax bill.

If you do not tell your insurance company you are letting and it only emerges after you have made a claim it could invalidate your policy.

Long letting

The basic provisions of a policy designed for letting properties will not vary that much from the policy which covers your own home. All the usual risks such as the effects of fire, flood and storm damage should be covered. As with your domestic policy, it is probably best to elect for accidental damage cover, though you may have to look around because many insurance companies will not offer it on let properties.

There may be exclusions if your letting property is left unoccupied or unfurnished for a period of time. Some policies will reduce cover after only seven days if the property is left unoccupied. The insurance company may also expect your gas and electrical appliances to be inspected annually by a suitable contractor (this is a legal requirement for gas appliances installed in a letting property anyway).

The other main difference between a policy covering your home and your letting property is the approach to theft. If your family home is burgled, there usually has to be evidence of a forced and/

or violent entry for your claim to succeed. However, in the event of tenants stealing from your letting property you have obviously given them the keys yourself, and therefore it is important that the policy is worded differently to cover this.

There are other risks which should be covered in your lettings' insurance policy. Check the points below are included, along with the maximum amount to be paid out on each:

- Lock replacements (if the tenants run off with the keys or they are stolen).

- Loss of rent (if the property cannot be occupied for any insurable reason).

- Legal fees (eg squatter or neighbour problems or consumer disputes).

- Property owner's liability (covers you if someone is injured on your property).

- Defective premises liability (covers you if someone is injured or something is damaged because of a fault in your property).

There are two further risks which are usually not covered by typical letting property policies and which potentially could be the most expensive of all:

- Insurance to cover your rent if the tenant defaults for any reason.

- Legal expenses cover in the event of a dispute between you and your tenant.

You can take out extra cover for these but it is more expensive. The rental cover could be around three to four per cent of the monthly rent. Legal expenses cover in the event of a tenant dispute is likely to be a flat rate of around £100–£110 a year.

You must take up tenant references before the tenancy begins. In the event of a claim the insurance company may want to see the references, and if you have not taken them up then you may have failed in your 'duty of care' and your claim could be rejected.

Holiday letting

It is usual for buildings and contents cover to be rolled into one which is logical. It would be odd if an insurance company only provided buildings and not contents cover for a holiday cottage since it clearly has to be furnished to serve its purpose.

Once again, the basic provisions will be similar to a standard domestic insurance policy so it is the extras which you should look at. Make sure your cover includes:

◆ Replacement locks.

◆ Property owner's public liability.

◆ Property owner's liability to domestic staff (if you employ a cleaner or gardener).

◆ Loss of rental income (if the property is unable to be occupied because of an insured risk).

◆ Provision of alternative accommodation (as above).

Some insurance companies will also cover loss of use of the property caused by death (accidental or natural causes), murder or suicide, as well as the pollution of beaches or other waterways within a set limit of the property (perhaps ten miles). A Foot and Mouth-type incident may be covered. If your property was officially quarantined (if it was part of a farm for example) then you would probably have a claim. If, however, you had no bookings because visitors had decided to stay away voluntarily then you probably would not.

Companies which cover holiday cottages may be more generous in how long the property can be left unoccupied before they demand from you certain actions (draining down systems, etc). They may also provide more extensive legal expenses cover than that generally offered for long letting landlords.

COUNCIL TAX AND BUSINESS RATES

Holiday letting
Most owners of second or holiday homes in England and Scotland are liable for council tax but will receive a discount of between 10–50% a year to reflect that the property is usually empty for some of the time. Each local authority has different rules, so check with yours.

If your property is available for holiday letting for 19 weeks or less a year you pay council tax. If it is available for letting for 20 weeks or more a year you pay business rates. This sounds like bad news but often is not because it can work out cheaper. Again, you need to check with your own local authority.

Long letting

If you long-let your property then the occupants will be responsible for paying their own council tax (unless the contract says otherwise) at whatever band the property has been assessed at. Speak to your own local authority to check if you are eligible for a discount between tenants. It may depend on whether the property is furnished or unfurnished.

12

What To Do If It All Goes Wrong

Let's start with some horror stories:

- Heard the one about the family who refused to leave at the end of their week's holiday?

- The couple who went out and left the taps running and the plug in the hole?

- The four year old who sprayed a bottle of black hair dye over a white bathroom?

- The plumbing virgin who tried to move a radiator?

- Or the family who stole all the pillows and left stained and mouldy ones in their place? (*Who* takes ten stained pillows on holiday?)

And the two cardinal rules to remember:

- Never become too friendly with your tenants or guests.
- Never lose your temper with them.

There will be times when you would like to wring the tenant's neck, when for example they phone at midnight about something that could have waited until morning or when a child has been allowed to colour in your walls with felt tips; but take a deep breath and *remain calm*. This is critical: do not become stressed, impatient or start shouting, because once a relationship between you and your tenant or guest has broken down it will be difficult to rebuild.

PREVENTION IS BETTER THAN CURE

Boring, but true. It is far better to put some effort into getting things right in the first place rather than having to resort to lawyers and the courts in the long run.

So, once again, make sure all references and credit checks are taken up before the tenant moves in, and make sure that a comprehensive, legally watertight Tenancy Agreement is in place. Also:

- Make sure your relationship with your tenant or guest starts well. Get this right and you are half way there already.

- Treat your tenant or guest as you would expect to be treated yourself, ie with politeness, consideration and respect.

- Pay attention to their requests, respond quickly and professionally, and if you are not going to do what they want, explain why.

WHO IS THE BOSS?

It is important right at the beginning to set out the ground rules. So you are the boss. It is your property and you are allowing tenants or guests to be there. You set the standards and state what is expected and it is up to the other party to either accept your terms or go somewhere else.

It is easy, especially in the early days of letting when you are still building up your confidence, to over-compensate and be too accommodating in order to keep a tenant or guest happy. So you may find yourself agreeing to requests which, with hindsight and a little more experience, you would not have done so, whether it be letting them keep snakes or painting the rooms green.

The vast majority of people are reasonable and responsible, but there will always be a minority who will exploit the situation if they sense weakness or indecision. So be firm but fair and prepared to hold your ground.

Keep reminding yourself that this is business and that you have invested in property to make money. What matters is the bottom line, and if something is going to cost you money or time then do not agree to it unless there is a good reason otherwise. It is no good wincing or turning fey at the mention of profit: you cannot have it both ways. You either do this properly or not at all (or become a charity).

HOW TO SPOT EARLY SIGNS OF TROUBLE

By picking up on potential problems at an early stage it may be possible to avoid matters escalating. Some warning signs are:

- The tenant's rent is not paid on time.
- The tenant damages the property or contents.
- The tenant steals something.
- The tenant is a nuisance to either yourself or the neighbours.
- The tenant breaks a clause in his Tenancy Agreement (for example, he sub-lets or keeps pets).

Or if the tenant is unhappy with you:

- They are dissatisfied with the property.
- They are dissatisfied with the management service provided.

So make a few early checks to ensure the tenancy is on track:

- Double check that the rent, deposit and any other monies are paid when they are due. Be suspicious of any cheques which bounce, bank orders which are returned or funds that are late. On the whole, these sort of things do not happen to well-organised, well-intentioned people. However banks do make mistakes. If it happens once give the tenant the benefit of the doubt but be on your guard. If it happens twice then act.

- Carry out an initial check on your property, perhaps a month after the tenant has moved in (having agreed this in advance). Continue with quarterly inspections.

- Consider making yourself known to neighbours and if appropriate, leave your number and ask them to call if they have any concerns. Tread carefully here though: good neighbour relations are vital but you do not want to encourage tale-telling.

And two caveats:

♦ Do not be over-protective of your property. No tenant is going to maintain it in a pristine condition for ever.

♦ A tenant has a right to 'quiet enjoyment' which means if you are found to have harassed the tenant you could be committing an offence.

Tenants may be pleasant, in a well-paid professional job, with a pair of charming children and a friendly dog, but this does not necessarily make them ideal occupiers of your property. The nicest people can live in the most astonishing conditions of squalor, but short of installing hidden cameras (not advisable) there is not much else you can do to protect your property.

VERBAL AND WRITTEN WARNINGS

Despite all your precautions things will occasionally go wrong. A bad tenant will, regardless of all the checks, slip through the net, or previously good tenants may turn into troublesome ones because a marriage or other partnership has broken up or there has been a redundancy.

Be compassionate and understanding if the tenant's circumstances have suddenly changed for the worse and they are genuinely in trouble, but there is only so far you can go. If they are making real attempts to resolve matters and you can see an end in sight then give them time. But there may come a point when you have to be brutal. Remember that if they cannot pay the rent you may not be able to pay the mortgage.

If you let through an agent then leave it to them to sort out because of course this is why you pay them. Otherwise it is down to you. And this is the point when you begin to see if you have the stomach for the harsher side of letting.

If the circumstances are really that dire you may want to start the process of trying to get your tenant out immediately. Otherwise it is probably best to issue a series of warnings, similar really to how an employer may treat an employee who is going off the rails.

One verbal and two written warnings should be enough for any tenant to get the message, no matter how dense or argumentative they are.

Verbal warnings

Be calm and rational. Beforehand, work out what points you want to get across. When you meet the tenant, explain that you are giving them a formal verbal warning, that you are not happy and say why. Tell them that whatever they are doing wrong must stop. Stick to those points and keep it simple. Give them a chance to respond and *listen to the answer*. Agree to review the matter in perhaps a fortnight or month.

If you think there is any danger of discussions becoming heated, then leave it until you or your tenant have calmed down. Then consider taking a third party (an agent or similar professional would be ideal) who could act as arbitrator.

Written warnings

So the verbal warning has failed and now you have to send a letter.

A warning letter should ideally be delivered by hand or sent recorded delivery, which gives proof of delivery. Again, you should say that you are not satisfied and explain why, and that whatever they are doing has to stop. Give them a chance to respond and a deadline. The letter should read something like this:

Your address
Date

Dear (Tenant's Name)

Re: (Address of letting property)

I am writing to give you formal notice that you must stop keeping pets/sub-letting/running a business, etc, from the above address with immediate effect.

Keeping pets/sub-letting is in direct contravention of the written conditions of your Tenancy Agreement, dated X.

I gave you a verbal warning on this issue on X, which you have so far chosen to ignore.

I must warn you that if you continue these actions beyond the date of receiving this letter, I will serve immediate notice on you to leave the property and may take steps to recover any damages or costs incurred from your deposit which I hold.

Yours sincerely

XX

If the tenant still continues with his or her actions, send a final written warning. The content will be similar to the above letter, but make it clear that it is a final written warning and that if they do not comply by X date, then you will start the process to regain possession of your property with no further communication on this matter.

Under no circumstances threaten the tenant with notice or any other sanction and then fail to follow it through. A tenant who was unscrupulous enough to break their Tenancy Agreement in the first place will continue to take advantage if they sense the smallest sign of weakness. And once you have lost control of the management of your property, you are doomed.

SERVING NOTICE

There is no choice here. You have to serve notice in the correct form: if you do not and the tenants refuse to go, then you will jeopardise your case if it ever gets to court. See Chapter Six for the procedure.

GOING TO COURT

This advice follows the English system: seek professional advice elsewhere.

Going to court is the last resort, when all your defences you so carefully put into place have failed. You have served written notice on your tenant to leave, but they have not done so and now you wish to regain possession of your property. If you have not let through an agent, this is definitely the point that you wish you had. Almost certainly, any well-established agent will have experience of the court procedure, and will not have the same emotional entanglement you may have as the property owner.

This is also the point where legal protection insurance comes into its own. Think carefully before refusing it.

Do you need a solicitor?

It is possible to go to court and represent yourself, but unless you are meticulous with the paperwork and have made yourself familiar with the process it may be safer to employ a solicitor. If any of the paperwork is not in order, the judge is able – and likely – to delay proceedings until it is. And it means that if you get it wrong you may have to serve another notice on your tenant which will cost you a delay of at least another two months (or longer depending on the length of the notice period).

So use a solicitor who has experience in these matters and who can be trusted to get the detail right. It may save you money in the long run, and will certainly mean fewer sleepless nights, grey hair and worry lines.

The court procedure

This next section assumes you have a correctly drawn-up Tenancy Agreement which is valid for a term of six months or longer.

If you want your tenants to leave within the first six months you have to go to court and prove your case in front of a judge. You will have to provide legitimate grounds for terminating the tenancy, and in turn your tenants will have the opportunity to explain why they think they should be allowed to stay. The judge will then rule after hearing the arguments from both sides.

After six months, from your point of view, it is much simpler. Assuming all the paperwork is in order, the judge *has* to grant you possession of your property. There is no debate.

Now for the qualification. The procedure for regaining possession of your property can be lengthy, and in practice it is usually difficult to get the tenants out within six months anyway.

The likely timespan

As landlord you will need patience and fortitude, especially when you begin to wonder if the current legislation leans a bit too much towards protecting the tenant. The process goes something like this:

◆ You serve your tenants with a minimum two-month notice to quit.

◆ They do not go so you lodge your claim at court.

◆ The other side has a chance to respond, usually two or three weeks.

◆ You go to court for the possession hearing. If it is within the first six months of the start of the Tenancy Agreement, the judge will decide the case on its merits. If six months have passed, you will be automatically granted the possession order. The judge will set a date for the tenants to leave. He will usually give them a week or two.

◆ If the tenants have not gone by that date, you ask for an enforcement order and the bailiffs are notified.

◆ The bailiffs will act within a fortnight or so, once their own paperwork is in order.

In practice it can be around four months from the point that you, the landlord, decide you want the tenants to leave, to the point where you actually regain possession of your property. And if you are unlucky, Christmas, Easter, the summer holidays or even Bank Holidays, can prolong the agony.

Some tenants will deliberately drag it out to the bitter end. Serial defaulters will not leave until the morning that the bailiffs are due, probably having enjoyed several months' rent-free accommodation.

From the landlord's point of view, one of the few bits of good news is that rent losses and legal fees are at least insurable, though the premiums are not cheap. See Chapter 11.

If you do not have a written Assured Shorthold Tenancy Agreement (AST)

If you agreed the deal with your tenant on a handshake, perhaps because they were a friend or family member, then you may not have a formal written Tenancy Agreement. If this is the case then (odd though it sounds) the situation does automatically default to how it would have been if you had signed an AST in the first place.

This is also the case if you do have an AST, but it is for less than six months.

What it means is that you cannot compel a tenant to leave within the first six months of them moving in (unless of course they are happy to do so). But after six months has passed, you can go to court and seek a possession order which *has* to be granted (assuming the paperwork is all right) in exactly the same way as if a formal AST was in place all along.

This is a complicated area, and if you are in this position for whatever reason then you should probably seek exact advice from an agent or solicitor with experience in this field.

If there is no AST because, for example, your tenant has been living in the property for years, then also seek professional advice.

HOLIDAY LETTING PROPERTIES

The potential for things going badly wrong here is probably not as much, if only because the guests have less time to do anything really bad.

But unfortunately, unless the house burns down or neighbours complain about noise, you will probably not know until after they have packed up and gone home.

It is usually best not to accept stag or hen parties, or indeed any group of young single-sex people, unless you are fairly sure they are the type to spend their days climbing mountains or bird-watching, and their evenings talking about it.

The occasional guest will write and complain *after* they have taken their holiday and returned home. Obviously always respond courteously, but it is more difficult to take these letters seriously because if there was a problem then the guest should have notified you or your agency immediately, giving you a chance to resolve matters at the time. It can sometimes be hard to see these letters as anything other than an attempt to get a refund.

Most agencies can go only so far in sorting out problems. Yes, seek their advice and call on them in the event of a dispute when a calming voice of reason from a third party may be useful. However it is almost certainly you who will have the contract with the guests, it is your property, and ultimately your responsibility to resolve any complaints.

Because there are no realistic checks you can make in advance on the calibre and trustworthiness of your guests, your only protection is a decent insurance policy. So make sure you take out a specialist policy designed to cover holiday letting accommodation and check carefully what is covered. The cost (not as horrendous as you may think) and what is typically included is covered in Chapter 11.

IF *YOU* GET SOMETHING WRONG

So far, only tenants' and guests' misdemeanours have been covered. Unfortunately though, unless you are super human, there will be times when you may be wrong. You could have forgotten to get the heating fixed, overlooked a broken door lock, or failed to make safe a garden pond. In those cases by far the best course of action is to confess, offer a dignified apology and then try to put matters right immediately.

Then there is the possibility of more serious disasters, including fire, burst pipes, burglary or personal injuries to tenants or guests. These may or may not be your fault, but in the short term that does not matter (blame can come later). What is important is how you cope with the situation.

Unless the circumstances are exceptional, always take the initiative. Remain calm and assess the situation. Decide on a course of action and immediately tell your tenant or guest what you have decided. Keeping them in the dark will not help and could make matters worse.

Once everything has been resolved, think about what went wrong and do whatever is necessary to lessen the chances of it happening again.

Remedies to offer

Obviously what remedies to offer will depend on the seriousness of what happened.

If you let through an agent, seek their advice on the situation and what level of compensation, if any, to offer. Starting with the least awful disaster, here are some suggestions:

- Apology and card.
- Token child's present, for example colouring books and pens.
- Bunch of flowers, box of chocolates, cake, bottle of wine or champagne.
- Partial refund of a month's rent or portion of the cost of the holiday.
- Entire refund of a month's rent or the cost of the week's holiday.
- A further month rent free or the offer of a free week's holiday next year.
- An offer to move your tenant or guest to another property for a period.

If you are in a position where you have to move your tenants or guests out then you should also be speaking to your insurance company.

Unless the problem is really serious, and the tenant or guest merits formal compensation, what you are doing is offering them a bribe to make everything all right again. There is nothing necessarily wrong with this if their equilibrium is restored and they go away saying nice things about you. But remember that under some circumstances, an offer of money or other compensation could be interpreted as an admission of guilt, so be sure you know what you are doing beforehand.

HOW TO DEAL WITH COMPLAINTS

During your career as a landlord you will almost certainly receive a few complaints. It is usually best to give the tenant or guest the benefit of the doubt, even if sometimes it means a Herculean struggle with your temper. So:

- Let them get their complaint off their chest, uninterrupted, no matter how unjustified or trivial you may think it is.

- If they are on the phone, consider meeting them personally. This will give them a chance to calm down, and most people are far less aggressive and unpleasant face-to-face anyway.

- If you are already together, get them into a one-to-one situation and away from anyone who may stoke the situation further.

- Do not lose your cool.

- Do not become aggressive.

- Do not let it become personal.

- Be aware of your body language.

Do not sniff at this last point because body language can make or break a situation. Be aware especially of the dangers of appearing to crowd your complainant, so do not get too close or in any way invade their personal space. If possible, keep your body relaxed, your face neutral and your voice quiet but confident.

If you think it likely a tenant or guest will threaten you physically, keep them on the end of a phone and do not go near them at all. Restrict all future contact to letters and give them notice to quit.

If you are threatened with violence or are physically attacked, do not retaliate and do not respond in any way. Get out of the situation as soon as possible, though it is useful if you are able to take the names and addresses of any independent witnesses.

If you are unlucky enough to be seriously assaulted (extremely rare) then you will probably have no choice but to call the police. Otherwise, give the tenant immediate notice to quit and make sure all future contact is conducted through a third party, whether an agent or solicitor.

13

Money Out

U nfortunately, the 'Money Out' chapter is likely to be longer than the following 'Money In' chapter.

Buying any property and getting it up and running almost always costs more than you think. And it is easy to forget the value of money: writing out a cheque for another £1,000 seems unimportant when you are thinking in tens or hundreds of thousands for the purchase price.

But because you are doing it as an investment, and presumably want to maximise your profit, it is particularly important that you keep track of your spending. Firstly, it helps you stay in budget and secondly, it helps you get your accounts right at the end of the financial year.

There will be big variations in costs across the country. A lot will depend on the size and type of property you are buying, where it is and how straightforward the purchase is likely to be.

BUYING COSTS

Buying costs are usually incurred in stages.

It is usual to be asked to pay for searches up-front: it is in case the purchase falls through and the solicitor or conveyancer is left with the bills.

Local authority searches

Expect to pay around **£100,** perhaps slightly more in large cities. Some searches' work is now farmed out to specialist agencies and they tend to be slightly cheaper, perhaps around £70–£75.

Water search

This checks the property's water and sewage arrangements. Around **£50–£55**.

Environmental search

This checks things like the possibility of air pollution, flooding or land contamination. If any of these are necessary, expect to pay anything from about **£50**.

Other searches

This will depend on the area where you are buying the property, but it could include checks for mining subsidence, perhaps another **£50**.

The next set of fees will usually have to be paid between exchange of contracts and completion.

Conveyancing costs

Expect to pay anything between about **£350** and **£800 plus VAT**.
You get what you pay for. It is possible to find cheaper deals, but
be suspicious of anything too cheap. If the purchase is likely to
be straightforward then a conveyancing firm should be fine. If it
could be more complicated or there are other agreements to be
drawn up simultaneously, then find a solicitor. Either way, it is
best to use someone local to the area because they will be
familiar with local quirks.

Mortgage lender's arrangement fees

Between **£500** and 1% of the loan for Buy to Let mortgages.

Mortgage indemnity insurance

Now rare: you should be able to avoid paying this.

Valuation

If you are buying with a mortgage your lender will want a
valuation. This is to confirm that the property exists, is saleable if
you default and will fetch enough to cover the loan. Depending on
the size of the property and where it is, expect to pay between
£200–£400, and anything up to about **£700** for a property valued
at around £500,000.

Survey

You will probably want at least a basic survey if the property is
more than a few years old. It is cheaper and less complicated if
the same surveyor carries out the valuation and the survey, so try
to arrange this in advance. For a combined valuation and survey,
expect to pay around **£500–£650** (not significantly more than the
valuation on its own). If, however, you want a full structural
survey this is more expensive, probably around **£800**, with the cost
of the valuation on top.

The National House-Building Council, or NHBC, insurance certificate covers most new homes which are less than ten years old. However the NHBC still recommends you get a survey. It has an informative website: www.nhbc.co.uk.

Land Registry fees

These are dependent on the purchase price of the property, and there are several bands. As an example, at the time of writing, the fee for a £100,000 property is **£100**; a £200,000 property is **£150**; and a half million pound property is **£220** (and **£700** on anything over a million, if you are interested).

Electronic transfer fees

Around **£30**.

Deposit

Ten per cent of the purchase price is payable on the exchange date, with the balance payable on completion. This is almost certainly the largest single sum of money you will have to find.

Stamp duty

Anything less than £120,000 is exempt from stamp duty. You pay 1% on a purchase price of between £120,001 and £250,000, 3% between £250,001 and £500,000, and 4% on £500,001 or more.

NB: Stamp duty is not a stepped tax: you pay whatever rate applies to your property on the whole purchase price. For example, on a £300,000 property you will pay £9,000.

Assuming you are buying an average house in an average area for £200,000, you will have to be able to write out a cheque for around **£25,000** to cover your initial buying costs (or more if your deposit is larger, which it probably will have to be).

SELLING COSTS

If you are selling another property to fund this investment
property then you also have to take into account the estate
agent's fees (usually between 1 and 3% of the selling price) plus
VAT. There will also be legal fees to pay, plus the possible cost of
keeping any furniture in storage.

AFTER YOU HAVE BOUGHT THE PROPERTY

The deal has gone through and now you have to prepare the
property for letting.

Redecoration

Budget to spend between **£1,500–£3,000** to repaint a modest two/
three bedroomed property and fit new carpets and curtains. It will
be towards the upper end if someone else does the work.

A new bathroom and kitchen start at about **£3,000–£3,250**,
including labour but assuming no major re-plumbing is necessary.

Removal costs

This assumes you will let furnished or part furnished.

A man with a van will cost anything from about **£75** for half a
day.

Moving the contents of a one-bedroomed flat a few miles across
town will cost a minimum of around **£250–£300**, plus VAT,
excluding packing and insurance, with a big-name removal
company.

Moving the contents of a three-bedroomed house across the
country will cost a minimum of around **£600–£650**, plus VAT,

excluding packing and insurance, with a big-name removal company.

If you want them to pack allow approximately another **£250**. (Recommended: they do it all the time and are good at it. They are also far quicker because they do not stop every two minutes to look nostalgically at old toys or photographs found in the back of cupboards.)

Insurance is quoted separately. Ask either the removal company or try to extend your existing home contents policy.

If possible arrange a move at the beginning of the week when it should be cheaper, and certainly not on Fridays, at the end of the month or during school holidays when removal companies are far busier.

AGENCY OR MARKETING COSTS

Depending on whether you decide to use an agent, you will either have to pay their fees or your own marketing costs.

Long letting – via an agency
- Agency charges: 'tenant find'   £75–£600
- Possible additional inventory, references and credit
  checking fees   £50–£200
- Agency charges: monthly management service cost
  per year (assuming rent of £600 per month and
  commission of 12 per cent plus VAT)   £1,015

Long letting – yourself
- Newspaper advert:
  local weekly paper, single insert   £15–£25
  larger evening paper, single insert   £35–£60

- Brochure design and printing (double-sided,
  full colour A4 sheet, including pictures) 250 copies*   **£300–£600**

*Anyone with a decent computer and a few ideas can probably
attempt a brochure themselves and save this cost.

Holiday letting – via an agency
- Agency one-off registration/contract fee   **£75–£450**
- Agency commission per year (assuming 30–40 weeks
  a year in an average cottage sleeping four, and
  20% commission plus VAT)   **£2,000–£4,000**

Holiday letting – yourself
Budget to spend about **£1,000–£2,000** in your first year, or about
ten per cent of your anticipated gross income, whichever is the
greater. If the website is an immediate success, then you may not
have to spend so much.

- Website set-up   **£500–£2,000**
- Website running costs per annum   **£100–£200**
- Newspaper/magazine advertising, single small insert
  in national newspaper travel section or *The Lady*
  magazine   **£30–£90**
- Brochure design and printing – see above.
  (NB: the more you have printed, the cheaper it is.)   **£300–£600**
- Tourist board membership, approximately   **£100**

FURNISHING COSTS
- Basic student property, two/three bedrooms   **£4,000–£5,000**
- Average family home, three bedrooms   **£6,000–£12,000**
- Larger family home, four bedrooms/two
  bathrooms   **£15,000–£25,000**
- Comfortable holiday let, sleeping four   **£8,000–£15,000**

RUNNING COSTS – LONG LETTING

This is where the differences between running a long let and a holiday let really start to show. By now you will probably have decided which one is best for you, but if not then compare the running costs of each.

Assume a two/three bedroomed property not in central London.

Annual bills

- Buildings insurance   **£150–£500**
- Buildings and contents insurance (if furnished)   **£500–£800**
- Additional legal protection insurance   **£75–£100**
- Additional rent protection insurance   **£150–£400**
- Servicing of appliances   **£60–£120**
- Service charges (usually a flat or in a complex) **£500–£5,000**
- Ground rent   **£50–£100**
- Accountant's charges   **£250–£600**

In practice most long-letting landlords, apart from those in London or the larger cities, will probably only pay buildings insurance, a bit to get the boiler serviced and accountant's fees.

RUNNING COSTS – HOLIDAY LETTING

One-off costs

- Phone connection (BT), if no existing line   **£75**

Annual costs

- Buildings and contents insurance   **£500–£850**
- Servicing of appliances   **£60–£120**
- Service charges (see above)   **£500–£5,000**
- Ground rent   **£50–£100**
- Accountant's charges   **£250–£600**
- Council tax or business rates   **£500–£1,500**

- TV licence (January 2006)   **£126.50**
- Possible chimney sweep   **£20–£50**

Quarterly costs
(Assuming gas or oil central heating, plus open fires.)

- Electricity   **£50–£200**
- Gas or oil   **£100–£300**
- Water and sewerage charges (you may be billed
  annually if you are not metered)   **£100–£200**
- Solid fuel, ie wood and coal   **£50–£75**
- Phone – monthly standing charge (out-going calls
  emergency only)   **£36**

Monthly costs
- Window cleaner   **£8–£20**

Weekly costs
- Cleaner   **£30–£80**
- Gardener   **£10–£25**
- Laundry. Bed linen for a two-bedroomed cottage   **£10–£25**
- Cleaning materials   **£2–£5**
- Loo rolls   **50p–£1.50**
- Welcome tray, including tea, coffee, milk and sugar,
  biscuits or cake   **£2–£8**
- Flowers   **£3–£7**
- Fresh soap   **50p–£1**

REPAIRS AND RENEWALS
Regardless of how you let, each year you will have to allow some
money for routine maintenance and, if furnished, for the
replacement or updating of some items. It is also a good idea to
have a contingency fund for emergencies.

Repairs

For newly-renovated, unfurnished long lets with a good tenant and for decent holiday lets allow about **£250–£500** a year. That will be enough to cover the occasional plumber call-out, touching up the paintwork and perhaps fixing a couple of window locks.

Renewals

For furnished long lets and holiday lets, you may decide to replace or update one big item a year: it could be a new sofa and armchairs, the beds, a bathroom or some garden landscaping. It will be far less painful financially if you plan ahead and spread the work over a period of years rather than do everything at once. Depending on the size of the property and the standard of fittings, allow about **£500–£2,500** a year.

Emergencies

You may want to think about keeping a separate emergency fund. If it is relatively easy for you to produce money quickly, then a separate fund probably isn't necessary. If however your bank account lurches from one overdraft to another and your credit cards are usually spent to the limit, then consider it. Most serious problems should be covered by insurance, but you could still end up paying some bills, at least in the short term. About **£1,000–£1,500** should be enough.

ADMINISTRATIVE COSTS

You will not be able to avoid doing some administration and record-keeping (if only to keep on top of your tax and receipts). The costs below range from a few phone calls and the odd letter if you have a long let run by an agent, through to a holiday let which you market yourself. If you do not have a computer, printer and scanner already, then consider buying them because life will be much simpler. Email in particular is just about compulsory if you plan to take bookings or will have any contact with the tenants or guests yourself.

One-off purchases
* Computer   £400–£1,500
* Printer   £50–£150
* Scanner   £50–£150
* Printer/copier/scanner all-in-one   £100–£250

Annual costs
* Printer cartridges   £30–£150
* Phone bills   £10–£800
* Stationery (plain paper and envelopes)   £10–£150
* Postage   £5–£150
* Christmas cards (for the previous year's holiday
  letting guests) plus postage   £30–£50

VAT
The threshold for 2005–2006 for VAT is £60,000.

If you are planning to invest in more than one letting property, especially at the top end of the market, it is possible you could breach that threshold. (It is based on the total income from the properties per annum, before deductions.) If you think this is a possibility then speak to your accountant well in advance of it happening.

CAPITAL GAINS TAX
As a general rule, when you sell a property which is not your family home or principal private residence (PPR) you will probably incur capital gains tax. There are ways of lessening your liability, including making sure you benefit from the annual exemption limit. If you are married you benefit from double the

annual allowance if the property is in your joint names, while unmarried couples can nominate one main residence each. There is also additional relief if the second property has ever been lived in as a main residence. If you are forced to live away from your main property for employment reasons, you may still be able to claim an exemption.

Get professional advice about your capital gains tax liability from the beginning. The situation can change from one year to the next, and each individual's tax position can be very different. There are many variables and delaying speaking to an accountant could be expensive.

14

Money In

There are two ways that your investment property should make you money. The first is through income and the second is capital growth.

Income

Income is simply the rent you receive from the property after all your expenses have been deducted. Some properties may be better at producing income if, for example, they are in areas where it is cheap to buy but where rents are relatively high. You will be taxed on any profit (over and above your personal tax allowance).

Capital growth

Capital growth is how much (if any) the property has risen in value since you bought it. A property likely to produce capital growth could, for example, be a wreck in an up-and-coming area which you have bought to renovate, or perhaps a property you believe is undervalued in an area which has continued good prospects for rising prices. The dangers here are capital gains tax (CGT) and possibly future inheritance tax (IHT).

Many investors hope for long-term capital growth because the income, especially in the early days, may be cancelled out by buying costs, large mortgage payments, and/or the cost of setting up the letting property in the first place.

Either way, the purpose of this chapter is to help suggest ways of maximising income while minimising the pain of incurring too much tax. But once again, if you are not sure what you are doing, then seek advice.

HOW THE SYSTEM WORKS

Virtually everything you spend on setting up your investment property (it does not matter if it is a long let or holiday let) can be used to help reduce your eventual tax bill. For example:

Year One:

Annual income from property:	£10,000
Less your expenses:	£8,000
Profit on which you pay tax:	£2,000

What happens if you make a loss?

Oddly, this can be a Good Thing, at least in the short term, because you do not pay any tax at all. You will probably incur many of your losses in the first year or so when you are setting up the property and furnishing it. This means that if your expenses exceed your income there is no profit to pay tax on.

Year One alternative:

Annual income from property:	£10,000
Less your expenses:	£12,000
Loss:	£2,000

Rolling over your losses

HMRC allows you to carry over your losses to the next financial year.

Year Two:

Income from property:	£11,000
Less Year Two expenses:	£12,000
Equals Year Two loss:	£1,000

Year Two loss:	£1,000
Plus Year One loss:	£2,000
Total losses to carry to Year Three:	£3,000

In Year Three you may not need to spend so much money on maintaining your investment property, so the sums could look like this:

Year Three:

Income from property:	£12,000
Less Year Three expenses:	£4,000
Equals Year Three profit:	£8,000
Minus losses carried forward:	£3,000
You pay tax on:	£5,000

If your expenses are high enough (and they will almost certainly be far higher than you imagine) you may be able to avoid paying income tax for some time. HMRC expects businesses to have a reasonable prospect of success. There is no particular rule on how long you can continue making a loss, but logic tells you there is little point having a property if it is not to make money at some point.

If you decide to switch between long letting and holiday letting on the same property, the losses cannot be carried over between the two.

WHAT IS AN ALLOWABLE EXPENSE?

Your losses are made up of two types of expense. Unfortunately you have to make the distinction because they reduce your tax bill in different ways.

Operating or running costs

These are anything you have bought or any bill you have paid which *maintains* your property. The cost of each item is simply deducted from your profit and you pay tax on what is left.

Examples include:

- Buildings insurance.
- Contents insurance (if you have furnished your property).
- The cost of repairing a washing machine or replacing a broken wine glass.
- Agency fees.
- Your accountant's bill.
- Mortgage interest (potentially the largest single expense). Note that you can only include the interest element of your monthly mortgage payment and not any capital repayment.
- Your administrative costs, for example a proportion of your home phone bill, paper, envelopes, stamps and printer cartridges.

- Journeys made from your home to the property, firstly when you viewed it intending to buy, and secondly when it is up and running as a business. HMRC usually allows a driver about 40p–45p a mile or a second-class train journey. You can also claim meals taken during the visit, within reason. (For example, if you live at the opposite end of the country to your letting property.)

If it is a holiday cottage, you can also include the following.

- The cost of employing a cleaner, gardener and window cleaner.
- Utility and other household bills.
- Laundry bills.
- Cleaning materials and items supplied for guests, for example flowers, milk, soap, tea and coffee, loo rolls and light bulbs.

Capital expenditure

This is anything you have bought or any bill you have paid which *improves* your property. Usually it refers to larger items, so a kettle probably would not be a capital item but a dishwasher or bed would be. Other capital items could include:

- The cost of building a new extension.
- Office equipment bought to help run your business, for example a computer and printer.
- New carpets throughout.

Capital items are treated differently from other costs because their value is set against your income over a period of time. In Year One you can claim 50% of what you spent: in subsequent years it is 25% on the reducing balance (2005/2006). For example:

Year One

Cost of item (eg sofa):	£1,000
You claim 50% of the cost to set against income:	£500
Leaving a balance of:	£500

Year Two

Remaining cost of sofa carried from Year One:	£500
You claim 25% of the cost to set against income:	£125
Leaving balance of:	£375

Year Three

Remaining cost of sofa carried from Year Two:	£375
You claim 25% of the cost to set against income:	£94
Leaving a balance of:	£281

And so on.

In theory, you can claim 25% of the diminishing balance on a capital item for eternity, but in practice there is little point when it gets down to a couple of pounds. Also, when a capital item (say a sofa or dishwasher) wears out, you buy another one which is also treated as a capital item, and the whole cycle of claiming first 50% and then 25% starts again.

If you benefited from using anything personally, then HMRC will expect you to claim only a portion of the cost. For example, if the total electricity bill for your holiday cottage for a financial year was £400 and you lived in the property yourself for three months and let it for nine, then you could only claim 75% of the bill.

When you sell the investment property you can use the purchase costs (legal fees, search costs, mortgage fees, stamp duty, survey, and so on) to reduce any capital gains tax liability.

It is also worth looking at HMRC's website at www.hmrc.gov.uk

HOW TO SET OUT YOUR EXPENDITURE

You can just give your accountant an envelope stuffed with receipts at the end of the financial year and let them get on with it, but it is far cheaper if you do at least some of the donkey work yourself.

It is a simple process, and essentially involves sorting receipts into the categories that the annual tax return requires, arranging them chronologically, sub-totalling each section, and ending up with one grand total of all your expenses for that financial year.

The categories for furnished holiday lettings are:

- ◆ rent, rates, insurance, ground rents, etc
- ◆ repairs, maintenance and renewals
- ◆ finance charges, including interest
- ◆ legal and professional costs
- ◆ costs of services provided, including wages
- ◆ other expenses.

The list for long letting will be similar.

Each accountant has their preferred method of seeing the information displayed, but it will probably end up looking something like this:

Date	Type	Item	Supplier	Cost £	Totals £
29/3/05	Finance charges	Mortgage interest	Name/address	4,944.00	**4,944.00**
10/8/04	Legal and professional costs	Accountant's fee		350.00	**350.00**
12/6/04	Other expenses	Guests' flowers		4.99	
19/6/04	Other expenses	Guests' flowers		5.50	**10.49**
17/6/04	Repairs, maintenance	Replace hairdryer		15.99	
14/7/04	Repairs, maintenance	Cleaning items		8.45	
11/10/04	Repairs, maintenance	Roof repairs		725.00	**749.44**
					6,053.93

Do a separate sheet for your capital expenditure items.

By far the easiest way of compiling this information is by using a spreadsheet on your computer, which will sort the categories alphabetically and by date order, then do the adding up for you.

You can do it all at the end of every tax year, but it is probably better to enter the data every month or so. That way you can keep a running check on expenditure, and at the same time not be faced with a truly enormous paperwork exercise by doing it all at once.

Obviously only claim for what you have spent. Do not get carried away in your efforts to reduce your tax bill. HMRC is going to smell a big rat if you claim the weekly travel expenses to clean your holiday cottage in Cornwall when you live in Inverness. Equally, you are unlikely to spend £10,000 a year on routine building maintenance or find it necessary to replace the tenant's washing machine every quarter.

If you are still thinking about whether to use an accountant, consider that a good one can save their annual fees and more by advising you of what is acceptable to HMRC (making sure you do not claim too much); presenting that information correctly; and ensuring that you benefit from all possible tax breaks. You are also less likely to face a detailed inspection of your books by the tax inspectors if you use a properly qualified accountant, although it is always possible you may still get picked up in a random sweep.

WHAT TO DO WITH YOUR RECEIPTS

When you are first setting up the property as a rental you will have lots of reccipts (especially if you are furnishing a holiday let), so you have to be organised. Old receipts look like rubbish to everyone else and they will be thrown away, but to you the receipts mean money, so look after them.

It is sometimes recommended that you number each receipt and then put the number against the relevant entry on the list of expenses. It probably does not matter as long as you can actually find the receipts if you are ever called on to back up a particular claim.

HMRC requires you to keep the receipts (and indeed all paperwork) for seven years.

OTHER METHODS OF ARRANGING YOUR TAX

Wear and tear

This is a far simpler method than above, but may be less lucrative.

If you are long letting your property fully furnished (ie it is covered by an Assured Shorthold Tenancy Agreement), you can claim an annual 'wear and tear' allowance. What this means is that instead of keeping a list of what you have spent, you claim instead a fixed flat rate of ten per cent a year of the rent you have received. In this instance, this is what your figures could look like:

Annual income from property:	£10,000
Ten per cent 'wear and tear' allowance:	£1,000
Less water rates and council tax (which you are allowed to deduct if you pay them), say:	£1,500
Profit on which you pay tax:	£7,500

This method is definitely quicker and easier, but do your sums carefully and decide which method will leave you better off.

Rent a Room

If the property is a student let in your son or daughter's name and they intend to use the Rent a Room scheme, then there is no need to keep receipts and prepare accounts. Under this, they are allowed to rent out rooms in their home (as indeed anyone can, not just students) and receive rent of up to almost £4,500 a year tax free. After that they still have almost £4,900 (2005–2006) in personal allowances, so in practice your student son or daughter can probably 'earn' slightly over £9,000 a year before any tax is due.

HOW TO SET OUT YOUR INCOME

If you let your property through an agent of any type, they should provide you with an annual statement showing your monthly rent received, minus any deductions (usually their commission plus VAT).

If you let the property yourself, then draw up your own statement (it is basically the same for long letting and holiday letting).

Date	Tenant or guest	Amount received (£)	Total (£)
1/5/06	Mr Smith	500.00	**500.00**
1/6/06	Mr Smith	500.00	**1,000.00**
1/7/06	Mr Smith	500.00	**1,500.00**

And so on.

Holiday letting just means you have rather more entries.

WHAT TO DO WITH YOUR INCOME AND EXPENDITURE DETAILS

You should end up with two separate lists or tables. One will be a record of what you have paid out and the second will be a record of who you have received money from. Each will have a grand total at the bottom.

Ideally you use the information to prepare a simple income and expenditure sheet, which just confirms your income was A for the financial year X, less your expenses of B. Then use those figures to either fill out your annual tax return or pass them onto your accountant who will do it for you.

Again, probably the most important thing is that you can back up any claim you make if the tax inspectors ever come calling. Being able to show them properly ordered expenses, clearly laid out, will look a lot better than frantically digging around in the attic for a box of crumpled receipts and some scribbled sums on the back of an envelope.

ROLL OVER RELIEF AND CAPITAL GAINS

A second or investment property usually incurs a capital gains tax liability. The amount is calculated on how long you have owned the property, whether you have ever lived in it yourself and how much it has risen in value since you bought it.

The principal method of postponing capital gains tax on holiday letting properties is to 'roll over' your investment into another holiday investment property. Basically this means that as long as you use the proceeds from selling one investment property to buy another, then you defer paying any capital gains tax until you eventually sell and use the money for something else. You can only benefit from this roll over relief on holiday lets and not other rental properties which are let long term and are usually covered by an Assured Shorthold Tenancy Agreement or similar.

PENSION CONTRIBUTIONS

Another significant benefit of holiday letting properties is that you can put a proportion of your net profits straight into a pension fund and receive tax relief. This is now the only form of saving which gives you tax relief, though the downside is that you cannot access the money until you reach the point you retire and buy an annuity. The proportion of net profits you are allowed to invest increases as you get older.

It is only possible to use profits from holiday letting to make pension fund contributions. You cannot do the same with profits from a property which has been long let.

OVERSEAS OWNERS

There are special rules for landlords who live abroad but receive rental income in the UK. If you let your property through an agent, the agent is compelled by law to collect income tax due on the rent on behalf of HMRC and only pay you the balance, although it is possible to apply for an exemption. If you live abroad, or are planning to do so, speak either to your own accountant or HMRC.

15

Building Your Empire

Increasingly, investors are not stopping at one rental property. Portfolios of five or six, or even 40 or 50, are no longer only the preserve of the professional or commercial developer.

Anyone with some money behind them (you may not need as much as you think), a bit of nerve, and some confidence in the long-term future of the UK property market, and of course the economy, can do it.

There are several reasons for this growth in property portfolios:

♦ Rightly or wrongly, many people still have tremendous faith in the long-term prospects of the housing market. In short, they think there's more money to be made there than in the stock market or in a savings account.

♦ Many investors are still nervous of the stock markets and the low points of the last few years.

♦ There is dwindling confidence in the pensions industry.

♦ It has never been so easy to borrow money to finance a property portfolio.

♦ Interest rates are still historically low.

Property also has an enormous psychological advantage over other types of investment. Everyone understands the property market and think they know a bit about it. Property is tangible, solid: you can go and look at it and touch it and, if you want to, manage it all by yourself. Compare that to a pension or a stock market investment, where events in New York, London or Tokyo, entirely beyond your control and possibly understanding, can wipe thousands off your investment overnight.

SPREADING YOUR RISK
The most basic investment lesson of all: *never* put all your eggs in one basket.

If you have one, your investment portfolio is probably made up of bits of single company shares, bonds, gilts, unit and investment trusts, cash, and so on, and in the same way your property portfolio should ideally be similarly diverse.

Yes, it may be tempting to buy up an entire northern terrace for the price of a semi in Chiswick, but what happens if your main source of tenants, for example a local company, goes out of business? Or if you decide to invest in rural holiday cottages and there is another Foot and Mouth-type disaster which all but wipes out the local tourist industry for a season?

If possible aim for a mix, perhaps a couple of long-letting properties, in town or country and for families or singles; plus a couple of holiday letting properties, one maybe in a seaside resort and the other up a mountain.

You may sacrifice some economies of scale by going for the scattergun approach, for example not being able to use the same letting agent or not being able to use the same furniture supplier, but the small amount of money you may have saved should easily be outweighed by the advantages of the spread of risk.

HOW TO BORROW MONEY TO FINANCE YOUR PORTFOLIO

There are many lenders out there now queuing up to lend you money to help build your property portfolio. Some will restrict the maximum number of properties you can own (to ten for example), while others do not care as long as the rent covers (or more than covers) the mortgage and that you maintain the monthly mortgage payments. Either way, you will probably be asked to declare how many properties you own and the lending against them.

Firstly and most importantly, as with any Buy to Let mortgage, you will have to show your expected monthly rent at least matches your monthly mortgage payments. In practice many lenders demand more, with monthly rent equivalent to about 125–130% of the monthly mortgage interest being about average. (For a detailed explanation of how all this works, see Chapter 2.)

Secondly, once you have met the above criteria, you can usually borrow up to 85% of the value of a property, though some lenders will advance less (perhaps 80 or even 75%) on more expensive properties.

As you will see below, the system works by re-mortgaging your properties and taking out the equity, or spare money, as property prices rise. The increase in value in one property finances the deposit on the next, and so on. You do not necessarily have to stay with the same lender throughout, but in practice it may be easier because you will know the system and what is expected from you, and the lender will know you. And some lenders are quicker and slicker at the further advances system anyway.

Interest rates on portfolio properties will probably be between one and a half and two per cent over base rate, and the mortgage company will want first charge on the property it is lending on. This means that when you want to take out the equity to finance your next property you either have to extend your existing mortgage or start again with another lender. What you cannot do is take out two mortgages with different lenders on the same property.

Before lenders consider you for further mortgages you usually have to show an impeccable six-month payment record, ie you cannot miss or be late for a single mortgage payment, or pay too little.

In order to make the transition (in the eyes of a lender) from novice to experienced landlord, only one rental property and one year's track record is usually required. This change of status can sometimes mean a slightly better loan-to-value ratio (ie you may be able to borrow more) and fewer checks on your personal circumstances (ie your income).

THERE IS NOTHING WRONG WITH BORROWING
(as long as you know what you are doing)

If you are serious about expanding your portfolio, you are going to have to get used to borrowing. You have to be comfortable with what you are taking on, and you must be sure you know what you are getting into. If you get into trouble, do not expect mercy from the mortgage companies because you are now entering the realms of commercial lending and will be treated accordingly.

In business, borrowing is perfectly acceptable, and in many cases it is better to borrow to expand than use your capital. This is an example of why:

You have £100,000 cash to invest in residential or long letting. How do you maximise your returns?

Mr and Mrs A do not believe in borrowing. They use their £100,000 to buy a brand new property for cash. They let the property for £600 per month, ie £7,200 a year. Because of inflation the rent increases and eventually, after fluctuations in the property market, the house doubles in value.

Mr and Mrs B use their £100,000 as deposits to buy five properties, just like the one Mr and Mrs A purchased, worth a total of £500,000. On this basis they also receive five times as much rental income, ie £3,000 per month or £36,000 a year. The other £400,000 is borrowed and they pay interest on this amount of five per cent, or £20,000 a year. Therefore, net of interest, they receive £16,000 a year. They are already better off than Mr and Mrs A, but what happens in years to come?

It is probably safe to say that Mr and Mrs B's rental income will rise with inflation in the same way as Mr and Mrs A's. However, Mr and Mrs B's mortgage costs remain the same. Therefore, the gap between both couples' rental income will continue to widen as time goes on. Then we need to look at the position when the properties have doubled in value. Mr and Mrs A have made a capital gain of £100,000 and have £200,000 worth of investment property. On the other hand, Mr and Mrs B have made £500,000, which is five times as much capital gain.

From day one:

	Mr and Mrs A	Mr and Mrs B
Property value	£100,000	£500,000
Mortgage	Nil	£400,000
Capital invested	£100,000	£100,000
Rent	£7,200	£36,000
Interest @ 5%	Nil	£20,000
Rent net of interest	£7,200	£16,000

Projection for 15 years' time, assuming properties have doubled in value and that rents have increased in line with inflation at three per cent a year.

	Mr and Mrs A	Mr and Mrs B
Property value	£200,000	£1,000,000
Mortgage	Nil	£400,000
Rent	£10,890	£54,450
Interest @ 5%	Nil	£20,000
Rent net of interest	£10,890	£34,450

(Illustration: The Money Centre)

HOW TO USE THE SYSTEM TO ACQUIRE MULTIPLE PROPERTIES

This section is for the determined few who want to do their own
calculations, otherwise leave it to a broker or financial adviser.

Let's assume you already own one letting property, Property A. It
has gone reasonably well and now you want to expand: you have
found Property B which you would like to buy. If you can
remember back as far as your school maths' lessons, the system
that will help you do this and build your empire is based on
compound interest.

The most important thing to remember is that you generally
cannot have a mortgage of more than 85% of the value of the
property. If the property increases in value you can take out
anything over this amount and use it to invest in another
property. This is probably the easiest way to work it out:

◆ Take the original mortgage for Property A
◆ Add to it the amount needed for the deposit for Property B
  (15% of the purchase price)
◆ Divide that total by 0.85, and the answer represents what
  Property A now has to be worth before you can extract the
  deposit needed for Property B and still leave 15% equity in
  Property A

It sounds far more complicated than it is, so try a couple of
practice sums yourself. It could look like this:

◆ You bought Property A originally for £100,000
◆ Therefore your mortgage of 85% was £85,000
◆ Now you want to buy Property B. The asking price is £120,000
◆ So you need a deposit of £18,000 (15% of £120,000)

So:

Take original Property A mortgage	£85,000
Add Property B deposit	£18,000
Total of what you need to borrow	£103,000

Therefore:

£103,000 divided by 0.85 = £121,176 (required new value of Property A)

You ask an estate agent to confirm Property A's new value, and you apply to increase your mortgage on that property to £103,000. This covers your original mortgage of £85,000, leaving £18,000 available for the deposit on Property B and still leaving 15% equity in your first property.

But no matter how you do your calculations, you will still need a cash stake to get started, either from your own savings or investments or perhaps from extending the mortgage on your family home if there is spare equity available. You will have to find an absolute minimum of 15% of the value of the property you expect to buy, plus an amount for legal fees, stamp duty, preparing the property for letting, and so on.

The only realistic way around this is to find a lender who will lend against the value of the property and not the purchase price. You then use the difference as a deposit. This means you have to buy your property at a discount which isn't as unlikely as it sounds. Buying off-plan from a developer (ie before it is built) can bring discounts. The developer wants cashflow and to be able to boast about how many units have already been sold. Buying through property investment clubs (PICs) can also mean discounts (groups of investors get together and benefit from negotiating bulk purchase deals with the developer or builder). Check out PICs on the internet anyway – there are plenty around. They are probably only worth considering if you are still thinking about multiple investments in urban/loft living/warehouse-style developments. But be aware that there may be regulatory issues with some (because they are investment vehicles, should they be financially regulated in the same way as others in the industry are?).

SELLING VERSUS REFINANCING

If you do not need to realise your profits for any specific reason (retirement or school fees perhaps), then there is an argument for refinancing. It looks something like this:

Imagine you had bought your Buy to Let property for £100,000 and had taken out an £85,000 Buy to Let mortgage some time ago. Now assume that as time has passed, both the property and the rent have doubled: the property is now worth £200,000 and you still owe £85,000 on your interest-only mortgage. You have three options:

1. Keep the property and keep banking the handsome profits you are now making on your rents.

2. Sell the property which will give you £115,000 less costs. But, unfortunately, you will have incurred a capital gain of £100,000 and the tax on this could be as much as 40%. At best, even if you have owned the property for at least ten years and claimed all of your indexation allowances, you will still have to pay £24,000 in capital gains tax. That means that you will have somewhere between £91,000 and £75,000 in your hand, which is still a good return. However the property has

been sold so you will obviously not benefit from any further growth in property values and rents.

3. Remortgage the property. Bearing in mind the property and the rent have doubled, you could double the mortgage. This would release £85,000 and the rent would continue to pay for it. You haven't realised a capital gain so there is no tax to pay, and you still own the property.

(Illustration: The Money Centre)

HOW MUCH IS IT POSSIBLE TO BORROW?

Some lenders set a maximum number of properties per borrower (perhaps eight or ten), others set a maximum borrowing limit (say £3 million), while others set no limit at all and it is down to personal negotiation.

WHAT HAPPENS IF PROPERTY PRICES FALL?

As everyone knows, property prices can go up, down, or stay the same.

Lenders ask you to put down a deposit of at least 15%, partly to allow for property prices to fall. Put simply, property prices have to drop by at least that amount before you fall into negative equity. And 15% is a big fall: many of the highly-publicised negative equity problems in the past happened to home owners who had taken out more than 95% loan-to-value mortgages which gave a much smaller safety margin.

But if you do not need to sell your properties, *it probably does not matter*. You may not be able to keep growing your empire if the prices do not rise, but that is all. You simply wait until they do again, as they surely must eventually.

The only two things that do matter are that you can continue finding tenants whose rent will cover your mortgage payments (over time the effects of inflation will reduce these anyway), and that you can sell the properties at a time of your choosing, if indeed you ever intend to sell.

DO LENDERS MIND WHO YOU LET YOUR PROPERTIES TO?

Yes, many do. Lenders often ban some or all of the following:

- students (some lenders accept students as long as they sign up to a single Tenancy Agreement)
- anyone on housing benefits
- local authorities
- housing associations
- asylum seekers
- corporate lets
- your own family members.

Lenders will also usually insist that tenants sign an Assured Shorthold Tenancy Agreement (or Short Assured Tenancy in Scotland).

WHAT TO BUY

When considering your options, think about whether capital growth or income is more important to you. Think as well about your time scale (the longer the better). Again, the critical point here is diversity. Spread your risk, and if one part of your property empire is flagging (no tenants or falling house prices), then hopefully another is more buoyant.

As well as going for geographic and individual property diversity, also consider a mix of the following methods.

Ready-to-let property

This is obviously the easiest choice and perhaps the quickest way of recouping some income from your new investment. Opportunities for capital growth are probably long term: any short-term capital growth would only come about if the property was too cheap in the first place.

Quick turn-around

If you are brave, have good organisational and/or DIY skills, have picked the right area and have done your homework carefully, then turning around property for a quick and profitable re-sale can still be a possibility even in a static or falling market. A decently decorated property, with perhaps a new kitchen and carpets, can do wonders in transforming something sad and tired.

Remember though that if you are considering this, make sure you include in your calculations the buying and selling fees, and not just the renovation costs. Legal fees, stamp duty and estate agents' selling costs can all add thousands on to your total expenses. It is probably safest only to go for a quick turn-around in a strongly rising market and where you are confident you know what you are doing. A project like this is for capital growth with no thought of income.

Renovation

There are more opportunities for capital growth on a renovation project, plus other potential advantages too.

By now you may well be an experienced landlord, with one or two properties already let. First time round you were probably not sure what your target tenant or guest wanted, or you were in a hurry to see a return on your investment. This time it may be different. You should have a far clearer idea of market expectations, and maybe a little more patience and confidence in your own decision-making. So this means:

- You can rebuild to your exact specifications, using your experience of what works, for example the number of en suite bathrooms or the quality of the fitted kitchen.

- You can pick your own time to enter the market, depending on where and when you see demand.

- You can add significant capital value to your property, as long as you buy at the right price and the rebuild or renovation is carefully costed and comes in on budget.

Land
Consider buying some land. You do not have to build on it: instead you keep it and hope it will increase in value. The thinking behind this is that there is only limited space in the UK, and such a shortage of new housing, that land prices must be inevitably forced up eventually.

If you are thinking about this, it is far safer to buy a plot which already has planning permission. Plots like these are advertised in local newspapers, via estate agents and via numerous sites on the internet. Access the National Building Plot Register via www.buildstore.co.uk.

If you are feeling brave, happy to wait maybe decades, and perhaps also a bit reckless, you could gamble and buy a plot without planning permission. It will be far cheaper, which is obviously the carrot, but there is no guarantee that you will ever get planning permission, even if you submit an application a year and live to be a hundred.

There are websites which sell plots in the green belt for those prepared to take the risk. Have a look at www.propertyspy.com and www.perfectplot.co.uk.

COULD YOU BE A PROPERTY DEVELOPER?

This is a very different career to just buying houses and letting them out, or sitting on plots. Some property investors decide to just develop a site and then sell on the property (or properties) as soon as the project is finished, and never go near any tenants or guests. And the financing structure on new builds is different because lenders usually release the loan money in stages as each step of the project is completed.

If you are considering this route, then you have two choices: either you can arrange the financing and sit back and pay others to do it, or you can be more hands on. This does not mean you physically build it yourself (though this would be an unexpected bonus): instead you take on the role of project manager. Most new builds, and indeed large renovations, ideally need a project manager. He or she will:

- Manage the builders, electricians, plumbers, carpenters, tilers and so on, and ensure they all turn up in the right order.
- Ensure they have the materials they need.
- Interpret architect drawings.
- Ensure the work is carried out to the correct specifications.
- Liaise with local authority buildings' inspectors.

If you decide to go down the development and project management route, you will have to learn a new set of skills (which needs another book to describe). First ask yourself these questions to decide if it is for you.

◆ Do you have the time? Consider that, depending on the size of the project, it could be an almost full-time job for at least several months.

◆ Do you have the experience? A new build or rebuild is nothing like a big DIY project. Do you know the difference between a first and second fix? When to call in the buildings' inspector? What a bung test is? Or a footing?

◆ Consider if it may be safer to have a third party between you and your tradesmen. Even mild-mannered people can be driven to murderous rage when the plumber does not turn up for a fortnight or when the builders stop to eat lunch at 10.30 a.m.

A competent and reliable builder can manage the project themselves, but you will be putting a lot of trust in one person. Also it is generally better to have another informed point of view for when things get tricky.

If you do decide not to project manage the new build yourself but would like to go down the development route, then ask your architect if they would take it on. If not, you will probably want to employ a surveyor or similar. Expect to pay them around ten per cent of the total value of the project plus VAT. A good project manager will earn their money by bringing in the work on time, and as a bonus may even be able to save you a bit by negotiating discounts on materials.

If you like the idea of development and think it has long-term potential, then the trick is to build up a reliable team. If you can find a builder, electrician, plumber, architect and project manager who are reliable and who can all work together, then do everything you can to keep them happy. It is probably worth paying them slightly more because it will save you money and grief in the long run.

MARKETING

Marketing your own properties becomes more worthwhile when you have a few of them. This is especially true of holiday cottages where you can set up one website and have a single brochure printed for all your properties. The significant sums you should save on an agent's fees or commission are more likely to make it cost effective and, depending on numbers, it could even be worth employing your own part-time property manager/assistant.

LONG-TERM TRENDS AND YOUR PORTFOLIO

For a brief period it looked like the opportunity to include residential property in Sipps (self invested personal pensions) would bring more investors into the market which would have affected supply and demand. In the end it was not to be (though it is still possible to invest in commercial properties such as shops and offices through Sipps).

Even if you are personally confident about the long-term prospects of the housing market and are happy to trust a large part of your pension provision to it, you still have to think carefully about what people's expectations of property will be in the future, both in the private rented sector and in holiday letting.

Even if property prices boom again, it is still possible to get it badly wrong if you pick the wrong properties in the wrong place and for the wrong reason. You may get it right first time thanks to beginner's luck, but with a collection of properties you have to go on making the right call every time (unless you have huge safety margins which generally means much larger deposits).

Long letting

ARLA (The Association of Residential Letting Agents) has reported that tenant demand in the private rented sector could grow by 40% in the next few years. It is being fuelled by the acute shortage of housing in many areas, caused in part by an increasing number of people living alone. Much of the tenant demand is from the first-time buyers being kept out of the property market by continuing high prices. Plus we live in a more transient society where people move frequently between areas and jobs, and who have to rent between buying and selling the family home.

So the long-term demand for rented property may be there but your profit margins may be a little less certain, if only because rising house prices generally mean falling rent yields.

Holiday letting

This is perhaps an easier one to call. There is little doubt that guests' expectations are far higher than they were a generation or two ago, when a spartan and unheated youth hostel or post war holiday camp was considered perfectly adequate for family holidays. Rightly or wrongly, we now expect a bathroom for every bedroom, a dishwasher and multi-channel TV.

And as people's expectations on quality are rising, so are their demands for flexibility. We want the freedom to take short weekend breaks, long weekend breaks, out of season breaks, or book for a week, fortnight or longer. And we may want to take our extended family or friends with us. There is an increasing demand for larger properties which will accommodate 12, 14 or even 20 people.

However, will the demand for self catering cottage holidays in the UK continue to grow? That is a trickier one, if only because they are often more expensive than a cheap fortnight in the Mediterranean, and the trend for rising personal debt means people have less disposable income. However what is not in doubt is that there will always be more room for *quality properties* coming onto the market.

Regardless of which path you choose, somehow you have to stay ahead of the game and anticipate trends. You also need some nerve, a good head for figures, research skills and a bit of luck. Have all that and you are well on your way to enjoying the benefits of a second (or third or fourth) property. Good luck!

Appendix 1
Checklist for Furnishing Your Long Let

ITEM	Approximate cost (£)	
Throughout		
Carpets, laminates and floor tiles	....	☐
Curtains, poles and blinds	....	☐
Lampshades	....	☐
Smoke alarms	....	☐
Carbon monoxide detector	....	☐
Fire extinguishers and fire blanket	....	☐
Reception room		
Sofa and easy chairs	....	☐
TV, DVD, video	....	☐
Coffee/side tables	....	☐
Side lamps	....	☐
Miscellany (cushions, pictures, ornaments)	....	☐
Table and chairs	....	☐
Per bedroom		
Bed and mattress	....	☐
Bedside cabinets (1/2)	....	☐
Wardrobe	....	☐
Chest of drawers	....	☐
Bedside lights (1/2)	....	☐
Mirror	....	☐

Kitchen

Cooker	....	☐
Fridge/freezer	....	☐
Microwave	....	☐
Dishwasher	....	☐
Washing machine	....	☐
Tumble dryer	....	☐
Toaster and kettle	....	☐
Pots, pans, roasting trays, grill pan	....	☐
Mixing bowls	....	☐
Lasagne, pie and vegetable dishes	....	☐
Crockery (dinner and side plates, bowls)	....	☐
Cups and saucers and mugs	....	☐
Cutlery	....	☐
Glasses	....	☐
Cooking utensils: knives, wooden spoons, corkscrew, tin opener, cheese grater, etc	....	☐
Vacuum cleaner	....	☐
Iron and ironing board	....	☐
Washing up bowl, bucket, dustpan and brush, inside bins and dustbins	....	☐

Total _____

Appendix 2
Checklist for Furnshing Your Holiday Let

ITEM	Approximate cost (£)	
Throughout		
Flooring	....	☐
Curtains	....	☐
Curtain poles	....	☐
Lampshades	....	☐
Pictures	....	☐
Telephones	....	☐
Waste paper bins	....	☐
Smoke alarms	....	☐
Carbon monoxide detector	....	☐
Fire extinguishers	....	☐
Fire blanket	....	☐
Torch	....	☐
Plug adaptor	....	☐
Reception room		
Sofa(s) and armchairs	....	☐
TV, DVD, video	....	☐
TV table or equivalent	....	☐
CD player	....	☐
Coffee/occasional tables	....	☐
Side/reading lamps	....	☐
Cushions/throws	....	☐
Video cassettes	....	☐

Games/jigsaws/cards .... ☐

Books .... ☐

Local Ordnance Survey map .... ☐

Visitor book .... ☐

Candles .... ☐

Fire guard .... ☐

Coal scuttle .... ☐

Log basket .... ☐

Per bedroom

Bed .... ☐

Duvet .... ☐

Pillows .... ☐

Waterproof mattress protector .... ☐

Pillow protectors .... ☐

Duvet covers .... ☐

Sheets .... ☐

Pillow cases .... ☐

Wardrobe .... ☐

Chests of drawer/dressing table .... ☐

Mirror .... ☐

Hangers .... ☐

Bedside table .... ☐

Bedside light .... ☐

Bedside clock/radio .... ☐

Spare blankets .... ☐

Hairdryer .... ☐

Hook for the back of door .... ☐

Kitchen

Fridge and freezer .... ☐

Cooker and hob .... ☐

Washing machine .... ☐

Tumble dryer .... ☐

Dishwasher .... ☐

Microwave .... ☐

Toaster and kettle .... ☐

Large saucepan and lid .... ☐

Medium saucepan and lid .... ☐

Small saucepan .... ☐

Non-stick frying pan .... ☐

Casserole dish and lid .... ☐

Roasting trays .... ☐

Grill pan .... ☐

Bread knife (serrated) .... ☐

Carving knife .... ☐

Carving fork .... ☐

Large vegetable knife .... ☐

Small vegetable knife .... ☐

Knife steel .... ☐

Small, medium and large Pyrex bowls .... ☐

Sieve .... ☐

Colander .... ☐

Cheese grater .... ☐

Corkscrew and bottle opener .... ☐

Tin opener .... ☐

Measuring jug .... ☐

Trivets for hot dishes .... ☐

Hand whisk .... ☐

Wooden spoons .... ☐

Potato masher .... ☐

Straining spoon .... ☐

Ladle .... ☐

Fish slice .... ☐

Spatula .... ☐

Serving spoons .... ☐

Kitchen scales .... ☐

Scissors .... ☐

Ice-cream scoop .... ☐

Tablespoon .... ☐

Potato/vegetable peeler .... ☐

Pastry brush .... ☐

Garlic crusher .... ☐

Salad bowl and pair of salad servers .... ☐

Fruit bowl .... ☐

Lemon squeezer .... ☐

Cafètiere .... ☐

Tea caddy .... ☐

Tea strainer .... ☐

Small bowls for olives, dips, etc .... ☐

Jug for fruit juice, water, etc .... ☐

Bread bin .... ☐

Butter dish .... ☐

Salt and pepper set .... ☐

Minimum two plastic chopping boards
  – one clearly marked for meat .... ☐

Wooden bread board .... ☐

Rolling pin .... ☐

Toast rack .... ☐

Tea towels .... ☐

Oven gloves .... ☐

Kitchen apron .... ☐

Serving and place mats, coasters .... ☐

Bin .... ☐

Dustpan and brush .... ☐

Washing up bowl .... ☐

Drainer .... ☐

Vacuum cleaner .... ☐

Broom .... ☐

Mop .... ☐

Bucket .... ☐

Optional kitchen items

Pestle and mortar .... ☐

Nutcrackers .... ☐

Vases for cut flowers .... ☐

Spoon rests .... ☐

Lemon zester .... ☐

Electric whisk .... ☐

Blender/liquidiser .... ☐

Steamer .... ☐

Wine rack .... ☐

Egg cups .... ☐

Egg timer .... ☐

Ramekin dishes .... ☐

Wine stoppers .... ☐

Knife block .... ☐

Steel and/or wooden barbeque skewers .... ☐

Mandolin .... ☐

Empty storage jars .... ☐
Cake tin .... ☐
Cook books .... ☐

Dining/tableware
Tables and chairs .... ☐
Dinner plates .... ☐
Side plates .... ☐
Cereal bowls .... ☐
Cups and saucers .... ☐
Tea/coffee mugs .... ☐
Teapot .... ☐
Vegetable serving dishes .... ☐
Milk jug .... ☐
Cream jug .... ☐
Sugar bowl .... ☐
Gravy boat .... ☐
Knives .... ☐
Forks .... ☐
Dessert spoons .... ☐
Tea spoons .... ☐
Wine glasses .... ☐
Small tumblers .... ☐
Large tumblers .... ☐
Medium plastic tumblers .... ☐

Bathroom
Bathroom cabinet or mirror .... ☐
Towel rail .... ☐
Toilet roll holder .... ☐

Toilet brush and holder .... ☐

Soap dish .... ☐

Bath mat .... ☐

Hand towels .... ☐

Shaving adaptor plug .... ☐

Pedal bin .... ☐

Laundry

Iron and ironing board .... ☐

Laundry basket .... ☐

Linen basket .... ☐

Clothes airer .... ☐

Pegs .... ☐

Babies/young children

High chair .... ☐

Cot .... ☐

Stairgate .... ☐

Selection of melamine/plastic bowls,
    plates, cups .... ☐

Cutlery .... ☐

Outside

Garden furniture .... ☐

Barbeque .... ☐

Washing line .... ☐

Dustbins .... ☐

Luxuries and optionals

Total _____

Index

accountants, 224, 227, 232, 235, 236, 237, 239, 241
accounts, 217, 238
administrative costs, 69, 226, 232
advertising costs, 69
affordability, 3, 31
agency charges, holiday lets, 4, 7, 66–7, 222–3
agency charges, long lets, 4, 7, 58, 222–3
agent references, 57
allergies, 120
annuities, 240
Any Questions, 145
arbitrators, 206
architects, 8, 256
Argos, 135, 172
ARLA, 8, 17, 113, 258
asylum seekers, 252

babies and children, 72, 80, 85, 89, 120, 122, 123, 125, 134, 136, 141, 146, 155, 156, 161, 163, 201, 202, 214
bailiffs, 210
Bank of England base rate, 29, 245
Bath, 43
bathroom design, 221
bedding, 122–4, 135, 148
bedroom furniture, 122
bicycles, 44, 157, 174
body language, 215
boilers, 9, 114, 164, 180, 182, 188
bonds, 34, 243
breakages, 103, 104, 107, 113, 140, 159
Bristol, 165

broadband connection, 44, 70
brochures, 192, 195, 223
   holiday cottages, 64–5, 70, 71, 79, 90–1, 257
   long lets, 75–7
builders, 8
building inspectors, 255, 256
bung tests, 256
burglars, 106, 175, 196, 213
business rates, 199–200, 224
Buy To Let, 1, 17, 22, 23, 26, 31, 41, 47, 49, 59, 167–8, 219, 244, 250

Calender of Compliance, 189
Cambridge, 43, 165
capital expenditure, 233–5, 236
capital gains tax, 178, 227–8, 235, 240, 250
capital growth, 2, 166, 229–30, 253
carbon monoxide, 97, 132, 143, 181, 186
Causeway Coast, 43
champagne, 92, 152, 214
children, *see* babies and children
Chiswick, 243
Christmas, 72, 89, 92, 101, 147, 153, 161, 210, 227
cleaners, *see* housekeepers
cleaning, holiday cottages, 116
cleaning/decorating, 12, 109–11, 116–18
commercial developers, 242
commercial loans, 16, 22, 28
compensation, 214
complaints, 214–6
compound interest, 248

computers, 44, 76, 174, 226, 227, 233, 236
contingency funds, 99
contracts, agents, 47, 68, 190–5
Corgi (gas), 180–1, 188
Cornwall, 42, 236
corporate lets, 19, 95, 111–12, 252
Cotswolds, 42
council tax, 4, 199–200, 224, 238
counter cyclical trends, 8
courts, 208, 210
covenants, 189–90
criminal offences, 179
curtains, 95, 96, 97, 110, 132, 221
cutlery, 95, 98, 131, 140

Daily Telegraph, 86
Denning, Lord, 180
deposits
　buyers, 30, 220, 245
　guests, 192
　tenants, 104–5, 191, 204
desks, 172
Devon, 42
disabled access, 112
dogs, *see* pets
Dumfries and Galloway, 42
DVD players, 80, 97, 124, 132, 151

Easter, 72
Edinburgh, 43
electricity, 4, 9, 183–5, 225
emergencies, 226
endowments, 30
equity, 26, 165, 166, 168, 245, 248, 249
estate agents, 39, 41, 49, 50, 55, 221, 249
evictions, 54, 102
Experian, 59

fax machines, 70
financial advisers, 18
Financial Services Authority

(FSA), 19
fire equipment, safety, regulations, 97, 119, 129, 132, 155, 186
fixes, 256
flowers, 92, 225
Foot and Mouth, 14, 244
footings, 256
four posters, 91, 124
furnishing costs, 9, 223

games rooms, 71
gardens, 4, 12, 35, 36, 37, 44, 47, 61, 75, 82, 89, 91, 104, 134, 135–6, 141, 148, 156, 157, 170, 186, 198, 213, 225, 226, 233
gas records, 180–1
gas, 158, 180–1, 225
glasses, 131–2
Google, 65, 82, 84
Gower Peninsula, 42
ground rent, 9, 224, 235
guaranteed returns, 9–10

Habitat, 119, 134
halls of residence, 171
hampers, 152
Hampshire, 42
Health and Safety Executive, 188
hen parties, 212
Highlands, 42
HM Revenue & Customs (HMRC) (the old Inland Revenue), 102, 177, 178, 191, 194, 231, 233
Homebase, 135, 172
Home Counties, 112
house price surveys, 39–40
housekeepers, 4, 63, 66, 118, 124, 125, 136, 137, 138, 139, 145, 147, 150, 154, 160–1, 198, 225, 233
Houses of Multiple Occupation (HMOs), 19, 174, 187
housing association letting, 10, 19, 41, 187, 252

Ikea, 134–5, 172
income and expenditure sheets, 239
indemnities, 57
indexation allowances, 250
inflation, 30, 252
information folders, 154–6
inheritance tax, 230
inheriting, 46, 168
insurance,
    Foot and Mouth, 14, 199
    guest deaths, 13, 199
    liability, 13, 157, 197
    pollution, 199
    reduced cover, 196
    theft, 13, 196–7
interest rates, 2, 14, 16, 21, 23, 24,
    26, 27, 243, 245
internet research, 18, 37, 78, 83, 87
inventories, 55, 58, 63, 102, 108,
    156, 191, 222
Inverness, 236
investment portfolios, 243
investment trusts, 243
Isle of Wight, 42
Isles of Scilly, 92

jacuzzis, 125
John Lewis, 119, 134

Kew Gardens, 44
keys, 103, 150, 192, 197
kitchen
    design, 221, 253, 254
    knives, 127, 147
kitchenware, 126–9, 135
Kite marks, 183

Lakeland, 135
Land Registry, 39, 60, 220
land, 254
Landmark Trust, 81
latex, 121

laundry costs, 4
Leeds, 47
legal fees, 98, 208, 235, 253
Liverpool, 47
loan-to-value (LTV), 23, 25, 245,
    251
local authority letting, 10, 18, 187,
    252
lofts, 47, 75, 250
London, 43, 47, 95, 100, 112, 165,
    176, 243

mailing lists, 91–2
management charges, 9
management companies, 41, 48
mattress protectors, 123
Mediterranean, 259
Monetary Policy Committee, 32
mortgages
    advice, 18, 31
    arrangement fees, 20, 28
    brokers, 18, 19, 20, 21, 31
    interest, 7, 25, 29, 32, 232, 236,
      244
    self-certified, 22
Motorcycle News, 86
Mourne Mountains, 43

National Building Plot Register,
    254
National House-Building Council,
    220
National Landlords Association,
    60
National Parks, 42
National Trust, 81
negative equity, 14, 251
neighbours, 52–3, 197, 204, 212
new builds, 255, 256
New York, 243
Norfolk, 42
Northern Ireland, 43, 100

off-plan, 30, 48, 249–50
Oftec, 182
oil, 158, 182, 225
open fires, 76, 80, 145, 155, 182–3, 225
ornaments, 97, 118, 163
owners' use, 4, 67, 194
Oxford, 43, 165

parking, 35, 36, 44, 46, 53, 75, 155
Peak District, 38
Pembrokeshire, 42
pensions, 240, 243
pets, 72, 75, 80, 106, 141, 161, 162, 203–4, 205
planning permission, 254, 255
Portable Appliance Testing (PAT), 184
portfolio
    building, 1, 27, 242–3
    financing, 244–5
postage, 227
printers, 226, 227, 233
privacy, 115, 148, 159
private water supplies, 188
problems, 54, 63, 70, 159, 173, 197, 212
professional developers, 49, 255
project managers, 8, 255, 256, 257
property auctions, 49–50
property investment clubs (PICs), 249–50

quick turn-around properties, 253

Radio 4, 145
ready-to-let properties, 253
receipts, 237, 239
recession, 14
relocation agents, 36, 40
remortgaging, 26–7, 251
removal costs, 221

renovations, 9, 253
Rent a Room scheme, 177, 238
rent
    arrears, 54, 57, 103
    controls, 17
    guaranteed, 9–10, 193
    loss of, 14, 197, 198, 211
    rises, 109
repairs and renewals, 226, 235
repeat bookings, 72, 90, 92, 117
Rising Damp, 17
risk assessments, 189
risk, 9–10, 168, 243–4
roll over relief, 240
RSPB, 86
running costs
    holiday lets, 224–5
    long lets, 224

safety, 179–80
satellite/cable TV, 44, 80, 124
scanners, 226, 227
Scotland, 100
searches, 28, 49, 51, 52, 218, 235
second mortgages, 168
security, 155
shares, 34
short/out of season breaks, 70, 85, 91
Shropshire, 42
Sipps, 257
sitting tenants, 17
smoke alarms, 97, 143, 186
smokers, 75, 122, 141, 161, 162, 171
sofas, 96, 121, 145, 171, 226, 234
Southern Uplands, 42
special occasions, 152
spreadsheets, 70, 236
stag parties, 212
stamp duty, 4, 9, 98, 220, 235, 249, 253

Standard Variable Rate, 26, 27
stock market, 2, 30, 243
Strangford Lough, 43
students
    bills, 174
    council tax, 174
    managing properties, 172–3
    neighbours, 175–6
    rent collection, 173
    security, 174–6
    summer rent reductions, 165,
        173
    tenancy agreements, 173–4, 252
sub-letting, 105, 192, 204
surveys, 26, 28, 49, 52, 219, 235
swimming pools, 36, 46, 71, 163
Switzerland, 82

tableware, 126, 130–2
tax,
    bills, 63, 223, 232, 236
    deductible, 120, 196
    inspectors, 237, 239
    relief, 228
    returns, 177, 235, 239
tea trays, 151
televisions and videos, 44, 97, 132,
    151, 158, 225, 258
Tenancy Agreements, 21, 30, 46,
    99–109, 191, 202, 204, 208, 209,
    210, 211, 238, 240, 252
tenant references, 55, 107, 198, 202
The Lady magazine, 86, 223
threats, 215–6

timescale, 7–9, 210, 252
Tokyo, 243
tourist boards, 83, 84, 87, 223
towels, 72
trading standards, 188

unit trusts, 243
upholstered furniture (fire regs),
    185

valuations, 27, 219
VAT, 227, 238
ventilation, 107, 183
visitor book, 133
voids, 11, 101, 109, 113

Wales, 100
warnings, 205–8
wear and tear, 237–8
websites
    costs, 69, 223
    holiday cottages, 64–5
welcomes, personal, 80, 150, 225
white goods, 44, 45, 95, 96, 98,
    125–6, 146, 172
wine, 92, 152, 161, 171, 214
winter letting, 161
wood stoves, *see* open fires

Yahoo!, 84
Yellow Pages, 173
yield, 5–7, 42, 166, 258
York, 43